NEW POETS, NEW MUSIC

new poets
new music

Edited by

JOHN SCHMITTROTH

and

JOHN MAHONEY

WINTHROP PUBLISHERS, INC.
Cambridge, Massachusetts

Photographs made by Richard Traub
especially for this book.

ACKNOWLEDGMENTS **Jacques Brel:** "Brussels" © 1968 by Dutchess Music Co.; reprinted by permission; "Old Folks" and "The Bulls" © 1968 by Hill and Range Songs, Inc., New York, N.Y.; "Brel" by Nat Schapiro reprinted by permission of Columbia Records, Inc. **Leonard Cohen:** "The Stranger Song" © 1966 by Project Seven Music, Inc., Division of C.T.M.P., Inc., 515 Madison Ave., New York, N.Y.; "Hey, That's No Way to Say Goodbye," "Priests," and "The Story of Isaac" © 1967 by Stranger Music, Inc.; "The Old Revolution" and "The Butcher" © 1969 by Stranger Music, Inc.; used by permission; all rights reserved. **Judy Collins:** "Since You've Asked" and "Albatross" © 1967 by Rocky Mountain National Park Music Co., Inc., New York, N.Y.; "My Father" © 1968 by Rocky Mountain National Park Music Co., Inc., New York, N.Y.; used by permission; all rights reserved; international copyright secured. **Donovan:** All songs by Donovan Leitch; "Atlantis" and "Hurdy Gurdy Man" © 1968 by Donovan (Music) Ltd.; "There Is a Mountain" and "Epistle to Derroll" © 1967 by Donovan (Music) Ltd.; "Mellow Yellow" and "Sunshine Superman" © 1966 by Donovan (Music) Ltd.; sole selling agent Peer International Corporation; used by permission; all rights reserved. **Ted Joans:** "In Homage to Heavy Loaded Trane, J.C." from *Black Pow-Wow*, by Ted Joans, © 1969 by Ted Joans; reprinted by permission of Hill & Wang, Inc. **Don Lee:** "Assassination" and "But He Was So Cool" from *Don't Cry, Scream*, by Don L. Lee (Detroit: Broadside Press, 1969), © 1969 by Don L. Lee; reprinted by permission of Broadside Press. **John Lennon-Paul McCartney:** "Blackbird," "The Continuing Story of Bungalow Bill," and "Happiness Is a Warm Gun" © 1968 by Northern Songs Limited; "Maxwell's Silver Hammer" © 1969 by Northern Songs Limited; used by permission; all rights reserved. **Joni Mitchell:** "Chelsea Morning," "Songs of Aging Children Come," and "Both Sides, Now" © 1967 by Siquomb Publishing Corp.; "Marcie" and "Michael from Mountains" © 1968 by Siquomb Publishing Corp.; used by permission of Siquomb Publishing Corp.; all rights reserved. **Laura Nyro:** "Hands Off the Man," "Buy and Sell," and "And When I Die" © 1966 by Tuna Fish Music, Inc.; "Stoned Soul Picnic" © 1967 by Tuna Fish Music, Inc.; "The Confession" and "Save the Country" © 1968 by Tuna Fish Music, Inc.; "Captain Saint Lucifer" and "Sweet Lovin Baby" © 1969 by Tuna Fish Music, Inc.; used by permission; all rights reserved. **Phil Ochs:** "The Crucifixion" © 1966 by Barricade Music, Inc.; used by permission; all rights reserved. **Buffie Sainte-Marie:** Words and music by Buffy Sainte-Marie; "Maple Sugar Baby" and "Until It's Time for You to Go" © 1965 by Gypsy Boy Music, Inc.; used by permission of the author and publisher. **Pete Seeger:** "Oh, Had I a Golden Thread" © 1959 by Stormking Music, Inc.; used by permission; all rights reserved. **Paul Simon:** "The Sound of Silence" © 1965 by Eclectic Music Co. (BMI); used by permission; all rights reserved; "Old Friends" © 1967, 1968 by Paul Simon: used by permission of Charing Cross Music, Inc. (BMI); all rights reserved. **Nina Simone:** "Four Women" © 1966 by Rolls Royce Music Company, 507 Fifth Ave., New York, N.Y.; all rights for the world controlled by Rolls Royce Music Company, c/o Walter Hofer, 221 West 57th Street, New York, N.Y.; used by permission.

CONTENTS

DONOVAN

JUDY COLLINS

TED JOANS

DON L. LEE

INTRODUCTION

What follows is a selection of poems which, if not uniquely gathered, is at least not typical. The poems are the lyrics of the new music, and the reason for this book is the belief, which many share, that these lyrics represent the mainstream of contemporary poetry.

In the world of art, particularly poetry and music, two phenomena have characterized the last decade. The first can be called a new renaissance, a spirit of aesthetic dominance that has given breath to men and women who, in a manner reminiscent of the 16th century, combine talents as poets, composers, and singers. The second is the almost complete failure of the academic world to recognize the existence of the work these artists have produced.

The end of the 1950s found contemporary poetry in America at a strange impasse. Much that seemed interesting continued to appear in little magazines or in the literary publications of larger circulations like *The New Yorker* or *The Atlantic*.

Another and often more promising strain of poetry was reflected in the descendents of the beats. The general prospect, however, was poor, and many critics registered the opinion that, for the time being, poetry in America, and lyric poetry in particular, was at a standstill. The effect on the recognizable intellectual scene was that both magazine editors and classroom teachers stayed with the preferences of publishing scholars. They all believed that the poets of contemporary record continued to be Stevens, Cummings, Auden, Eliot, and Pound. Occasional efforts to include such poets as John Wain or George Barker faltered. The texts of the extended beats like Ginsberg, or even Brother Antoninus, proved too esoteric. As had happened before in literary history, literature appeared to have taken solely a prose direction, academically. The contemporary world was reflected in new courses developed around fiction, and the study of contemporary poetry relapsed again to "modern." Courses so designated began with the Georgians and culminated in the effect of Eliot on the present, with much attention—deservedly—to Stevens, Williams, Frost, and Cummings.

Of the sound of the new poets, the first that academicians—teachers—might have heard was the one the Beatles made. But, understandably, teachers did not. Other work of merit no doubt preceded the Beatles', but it was perhaps a step short of art or a step short of confidence. It seems unquestionable that the musical heritage of the Beatles and those groups that have followed them was rock. There are many good studies of this idea. But not all the new poets of the new music derive from the rock tradition. Nor, in fact, do the poetic achievements of John Lennon and Paul McCartney stem from rock alone—and neither do those of Joni Mitchell, David Crosby, Steve Stills, Donovan, or Leonard Cohen.

One should interpose that for three or four decades before the sixties slender ·but very strong threads existed that made this colorful tapestry of the new renaissance possible. Jazz, of course, was alive and well and moving steadily toward an ultimate music. Its direction was consistently toward the "cool," the intellectual, rivaling in complexity modern poetry itself. Charlie "Bird" Parker, Miles Davis, Dizzy Gillespie, and the great "Trane"—John Coltrane—were soaring to what seemed a quintessential jazz. (An interesting sidelight is the direct influence of this music on certain areas of the new poetry. Both Ted Joans and Don Lee have close ties with jazz. Joans was himself a jazz musician. And Don Lee, in public readings of his own poetry, imitates the rhythms and even the runs of Coltrane—sustaining vowel sounds, utilizing intricate "Trane"-like repetitions and rhythms.)

Both the blues and folk music, which frequently merged, were very much alive. For many of us, two names bring back the magic of the forties—Ella Fitzgerald, she of the immaculate phrasing, and the great Mr. B., Billy Eckstein. Otis Redding, generally acknowledged a father of Soul, came directly out of the blues tradition.

Too, the unlikely couple of Leadbelly—Huddie Ledbetter—and Woody Guthrie founded much of what is now described as "new folk." (Again, there is an interesting direct link with the present. Arlo Guthrie's sensational "Alice's Restaurant" is, in form, a "talking blues," a mode his father perfected in the thirties.) In this context, one must acknowledge Pete Seeger who not only nourished folk music, but demonstrated very early in his work with the Weavers the level of artistry of which a group was capable.

The complexity, the intellectual and artistic level of modern jazz provided an excellence to which today's lyricist, the new young poet, could aspire. The blues touched his heart and provided two of his major themes—alienation and loneliness. Folk music, particularly the music of protest, made Bob Dylan possible. And the artistry of such groups as the Weavers was no small influence on the achievement of the many excellent groups today.

As casual and incomplete as this record is, it makes clear that today's artists, both the poets represented here and others, have a solid basis for their shared but implicit understanding that poetry and music can always be one; they share, too, a working success in demonstrating that understanding.

The result—the lyric productions of these groups and these many-talented individuals —is not only a genuine contribution to the history of English poetry but perhaps also one of the milestones in the continuity of English poetry.

That which derives, in the poems in this book, from the traditions of English poetry must be left to the discernments of others. Some of the essays included here may help. What is most important from the editors' and authors' point of view is asserting that such a collection as this is not genuflection to a fad. For one thing, it should be obvious to anyone who lived through the forties that the lyrics of popular songs in that decade—or the decades before and after, for that matter—could not have been anthologized. The moon-June tunes, the Tin-Pan Alley world, dominated this work. But for reasons that only another essay might elaborate, popular music in the sixties turned real. Those who wrote it, those who played it, and, surprisingly, those who peddled it dealt with art. One of the ironies of disbelief in its work, indeed, is that its commercial success and wide popularity fended off the critics, the teachers, and the scholars. They were justified in a preliminary way; before them, nothing much that made money had been very good. Other things contributed to their diffidence, though. The new poetry-new music tends to be played too loudly, for one. For another, like most instrumentally sophisticated music, the words require a diligent ear for quick intelligibility. For a third, and an important one, the new poets tend to outdo the Lost Generation. Their political beliefs put some people off. Their generalized aesthetic concerns make their personal habits too often alien to academicians. Before their music was heard, the first and chief reaction to the

Beatles, for instance, was to their hair. As a result, perhaps, as few teachers can quote Lennon-McCartney as students can quote, say, John Barth.

All arguments aside, it is at least a reasonable notion that the new poets and musicians are carrying the tradition of English poetry more than anyone else. The highly traditional (though almost medieval) work of Leonard Cohen suggests that this is so. The gentle prophecies and inexpressible lyricism of Donovan suggest it. The romantic (almost Romantic) plaints of Joni Mitchell suggest it. The disciplined and formalistic poems of John Lennon-Paul McCartney suggest it. And so does the theologically tuned sound of Laura Nyro.

This having been asserted and all other things said, it seems fitting to exit with a line from Donovan that may be more to the point than all our comments. In a preface to "Phonograph Record/The First," which he signed "Thy humble minstrel," Donovan concludes:

I do hope you enjoy my new writings.

It seems important to assure you that we, too, most earnestly do hope you enjoy all these new writings.

Your humble editors,
J.S., J.M.

JACQUES BREL

BRUSSELS

It was the time when Brussels could sing
It was the time of the silent movies
It was the time when Brussels was king
It was the time when Brussels bustled

Pick out a hat so dashing and gay
Go take a walk it's a beautiful day
Put on your spats and your high-button shoes
Get on the tram get the gossip and news

Not a time for crying
How the heart was flying

There was my grandfather
There was my grandmother
He was a young soldier
She was so much bolder
He had no brains
Neither did she
How bright could I turn out to be

It was the time when Brussels could sing
It was the time of the silent movies
It was the time when Brussels was king
It was the time when Brussels bustled

Pick out a dress so dashing and gay
Go out and dance it's a beautiful day
Dance in your spats and your high-button shoes
Dance on the tram get the gossip and news

Not a time for crying
How the heart was flying
There was my grandfather
There was my grandmother
He knew how to do it
And she let him do it
They lived in sin
Deliciously
Now they prolong my virginity

It was the time when Brussels could sing
It was the time of the silent movies
It was the time when Brussels was king
It was the time when Brussels bustled

Sing out a song so dashing and gay
Walk hand in hand it's a beautiful day
Hop on the tram in your high-button shoes
Dance on the tram to the gossip and news

Not a time for crying
How the heart was flying
There was my grandfather
There was my grandmother

Ten million guns got loaded
World War One exploded
It was such fun
Whee what a game
They saved the world but I bring it shame

It was the time when Brussels could sing
It was the time of the silent movies
It was the time when Brussels was king
It was the time when
It was the time when
It was the time when Brussels could sing
It was the time of the silent movies
It was the time when Brussels was king
It was the time when
                        Brussels
                              bustled

OLD FOLKS

The old folks don't talk much
And they talk so slowly when they do
They are rich they are poor
Their illusions are gone
They share one hearth or two

Their homes all smell of time
Of old photographs of an old-fashioned song
Though you may live in town
You live so far away
When you've lived too long

And have they laughed too much
Do their dry voices crack talking of times gone by
And have they cried too much
A tear or two still always
Seems to cloud the eye

They watch the old silver clock
When day is through
It tick-tocks so slow
It says yes it says no
It says "I'll wait for you"

The old folks dream no more
The books have gone to sleep
The piano's out of tune
The little cat is dead
And no more do they sing
On Sunday afternoon

The old folks move no more
Their world has become too small
Their bodies feel like lead
They might look out a window
Or else sit in a chair
Or else they stay in bed

And if they still go out
Arm in arm arm in arm
In the morning chill
It's to have a good cry
To say their last goodbye
To one who's older still

And then they go home
To their old silver clock
When day is through
It tick-tocks so slow
It says yes it says no
It says "I'll wait for you"

The old folks never die
They just put down their heads
And go to sleep one day
They hold each other's hand
Like children in the dark
But one will get lost anyway

6   JACQUES BREL

And the other will remain
Just sitting in that room
Which makes no sound
It doesn't matter now
The sound has died away
And echoes all around

You'll see them when they walk
Through the sun-filled park
Where children run and play
It hurts too much to smile
It hurts too much but life
Goes on for still another day

As they try to escape
The old silver clock
When day is through
It tick-tocks so slow
It says yes it says no
It says "I'll wait for you"

The old silver clock
That's hanging on the wall
That waits for us all

THE BULLS

On Sundays
The bulls get so bored
When they are asked
To show off for us

There is the sun, the sand and the arena
There are the bulls ready to bleed for us

It's the time when grocery clerks

Become Don Juan
It's the time when all ugly girls
Turn into swans
Ah

Who can say of what he's found
That bull who turns and paws the ground
And suddenly he sees himself in the nude
Ah
Who can say of what he dreams
That bull who hears the silent screams
From the open mouth of multiudes

On Sundays
The bulls get so bored
When they are asked
To suffer for us

There are the picadors and the mob's revenge
There are the toreros and the mob kneels for us

It's the time when grocery clerks
Become Garcia Lorca
And the girls put roses in their teeth
Like Carmen
(Olé olé to madre to padre olé)

On Sundays
The bulls get so bored
When they are asked
To drop dead for us

The sword will plunge down and the mob will drool
The blood will pour down and turn the sand to mud

The moment of triumph when grocery clerks
Become Nero
The moment of triumph when the girls scream and shout
The name of a hero
Ah

And when finally they fell
Did the bulls dream of a hell
Where men and worn-out matadors still burn
Or perhaps with their last breaths
Would they not pardon us their deaths
Knowing what we did
At Carthage (olé)
Waterloo (olé)
Verdun (olé)
Stalingrad (olé)
Iwo Jima (olé)
Hiroshima (olé)
SAIGON

BREL   Nat Schapiro

Jacques Brel's slight figure—not quite perpendicular to the stage—awkwardly adjusts itself to the frightening fact of an audience *out there*. Upon his face there may very well be a sheepish, somewhat quizzical grin, exposing an unashamed array of incipient buck teeth. Not even remotely does he resemble a man who commands the adulation of millions and the profound respect of the poets and intellectuals of all of France.

But the moment he begins to sing his songs, something wonderful happens, and it goes on happening and happening and happening until both Brel and his congregation have completed an exalted and nightmarish tour of heaven and hell.

It began happening in Belgium in 1929 when his first (unrecorded) plaints were aired. Upon reaching maturity, young Brel decided to forego the security and comforts of a family business with an assured income and, guitar in hand, fled Flanders' fields for the unrestricted freedom that only Paris can offer to the restless, creative spirit.

Under the auspices of an astute impresario named Jacques Canetti, Brel began to attract attention during an engagement at the Théâtre des Trois Baudets, a small showcase for new talent just off boulevard Clichy in the Pigalle section of Paris. Slowly, his reputation grew, until each new recording, each new appearance in the music halls of Paris became a major social and cultural event. By the early 1960s,

Jacques Brel had become the ranking writer-composer-interpreter of meaningful modern songs in France.

Jacques Brel fiercely insists that he is *not* a poet and that he cannot, in fact, write verse, that it is impossible for him to imagine or visualize or write words without the sound of music intruding. If we should accept his denial, then we must indeed find a new and very special classification for his art.

Certainly Brel's lyrics are closer to poetry than almost all the cheap doggerel manufactured by the mini-minds of all the tin-pan alleys of the Western world. His burning imagery, his brilliantly controlled rhythmic patterns, and his superb sense of dramatic construction are the marks of not only the craftsman but the artist.

It is part of a tradition. In simple truth, no popular music In modern times can match the French *chanson* for its maturity, literacy, and purity.

Perhaps it started with the troubadours, or maybe with François Villon. Certainly, in modern times, we know that Aristide Bruant, celebrated in the *fin de siècle* drawings of Toulouse-Lautrec, was the founder of the contemporary school of French popular songwriting. Bruant—he of the black wide-brimmed hat, the brilliant long red scarf, and the highly polished hip boots—began writing, composing, and singing his songs in Montmartre at the turn of the century. At his café concerts, he sang of conscripts, whores, and pimps, of convicts and cops, to audiences made up not only of conscripts, whores, pimps, convicts, and cops but also of artists and writers and even politicians. His language echoed the sounds of the streets, his tunes were raucously gay and sadly simple. The people of Paris sang along with him and the poets paid heed.

The French do not flinch at the word "poetry" and their popular entertainers more often than not have in their repertoires lyrics by such esteemed writers as Jean Paul Sartre, Jacques Prevert, Louis Aragon, Jean Cocteau, Raymond Queneau, and dozens of others who find nothing at all demeaning in the creating of popular songs. Further, many of France's leading popular composers have successfully set to music works of such classic and modern masters as Verlaine, Rimbaud, Baudelaire, Hugo, Apollinaire, Ronsard, de Musset, and—back to the womb—Villon.

Brel, then, while certainly phenomenal, is hardly a phenomenon . . . merely part of a quite glorious tradition.

Brel first entered into American focus in 1957 when this writer, then employed by Columbia Records, returned from Paris with tapes of some of Brel's earliest works and a fervent determination to spread the gospel. A long-playing album, *American Debut,* was released, quickly devoured by a very small group of aficionados, and then, when sales diminished, taken out of circulation.

At that time, poet-playwright Eric Blau was putting together a topical off-Broadway revue, cryptically entitled "O, Oysters!," for presentation at the Village Gate in New York. Two of Brel's songs, "Ne me quitte pas" and the unbelievable *tour de* force "La Valse à mille temps," were adapted by Blau for his show, in which they were sung with stunning effect by enchanting Elly Stone. After a considerable run, "O, Oysters!" closed, but Miss Stone, in concerts and in supper clubs, continued to sing the Brel songs, never failing to elicit extraordinary audience response.

Quite independently, in the early 1960s, Mort Shuman, who had been enjoying enormous success as a composer of popular music, principally of the rhythm-and-blues genre, met Brel in Paris and became not only a disciple but also a friend of the singer-composer. Disenchanted with some of the adaptations of his songs that had begun appearing on American records, Brel entrusted Shuman with a number of his most important works.

Early in 1967, Eric Blau and I, en route to a musical disaster in Philadelphia, decided that it would be a lovely idea to present Brel's work in some sort of theatrical form, and we began plotting ways and means of putting together a show. A meeting with Mort Shuman seemed called for and was arranged. It was immediately evident that Blau's poetic gifts and Shuman's polished craftsmanship, supplemented by their mutual love and understanding of what Jacques Brel is all about, would yield exciting rewards.

After choosing the brilliant young Israeli mime-actor-director Moni Yakim to stage the production, it was a foregone conclusion that Elly Stone had to take part. Then Shuman, who had been demonstrating his songs with devastating effect to prospective backers, was persuaded to relinquish the protection of his piano and display his formidable physical presence, voice, dramatic ability, and gorgeous sideburns to the paying customers. A pair of gifted singers named Alice Whitfield and Shawn Elliott were invited to join in—and casting was completed.

For the record, Jacques Brel is very alive and very well and living (very nicely, thank you) in Paris. His strong feeling about America's participation in the war in Vietnam has expressed itself in his reluctance to work in the United States. (He has appeared here only twice—to capacity audiences at Carnegie Hall.) Further, and terribly distressing to his admirers everywhere, he has announced that he will no longer make concert appearances. For the time being, anyway.

We can only hope that he changes his mind, for no one else on earth can do what Brel does. No one else on earth can compose and write and sing as consistently and as brilliantly as he can. Until now, most of his songs were either completely unknown here or they have defied adaptation. But, as we joyously discover in the entertainment "Jacques Brel Is Alive and Well and Living in Paris," Brel, unlike certain delicate French wines, can travel. When handled with passion and intelligence, his message can be distinctly heard in English. His songs, in the Blau-Shuman versions, maintain their power, their ability to shock, amuse, penetrate, wound, and arouse. They happen. They are, to be sure, some of the most dazzling examples of what is happening in popular music throughout the world today.

LEONARD COHEN

THE BUTCHER

I came upon a butcher
He was slaughtering a lamb
I accused him there
With his tortured lamb
He said, "Listen to me, child
I am what I am
And you, you are my only son."

Well, I found a silver needle
I put it into my arm
It did some good
Did some harm.
But the nights were cold

And it almost kept me warm
How come the night is long?

I saw some flowers growing up
Where that lamb fell down
Was I supposed to praise my lord
Make some kind of joyful sound?
He said, "Listen, listen to me now
I go round and round,
And you, you are my only child."

Do not leave me now,
Do not leave me now,
I'm broken down
From a recent fall.
Blood upon my body
And ice upon my soul
Lead on, my son, it is your world.

THE STRANGER SONG

It's true that all men you knew
Were dealers who said they were through
With dealing every time you gave them shelter
I know that kind of man
It's hard to hold the hand of anyone
Who's reaching for the sky just to surrender.
Who's reaching for the sky just to surrender.

And then sweeping up the jokers that he left behind
You find he did not leave you very much
Not even laughter
Like any dealer, he was watching for the card that is so high and wild
He'll never need to deal another
He was just some Joseph looking for a manger
He was just some Joseph looking for a manger.

And then leaning on your window sill
He'll say one day you caused his will
To weaken with your love and warmth and shelter
And then taking from his wallet
   an old schedule of trains, he'll say,
"I told you when I came I was a stranger,
I told you when I came I was a stranger."

But now another stranger
Seems to want to ignore his dreams
As though they were the burden of some other
O, you've seen that kind of man before
His golden arm dispatching cards
But now it's rusted from the elbow to the finger
Yes, he wants to trade the game he knows for shelter.

You hate to watch another tired man
   lay down his hand, like he was
   giving up the holy game of poker
And while he talks his dreams to sleep
You notice there's a highway that is
   curling up like smoke above his shoulder,
It's curling up like smoke above his shoulder.

You tell him to come in sit down
But something makes you turn around
The door is open, you can't close your shelter
You try the handle of the road
It opens, do not be afraid
It's you my love, you who are the stranger
It is you my love, you who are the stranger.

Well, I've been waiting, I was sure
We'd meet between the trains we're waiting for
I think it's time to board another
Please understand, I never had a secret chart
To get me to the heart
Of this or any other matter
When he talks like this
   you don't know what he's after
When he speaks like this
   you don't know what he's after.

Let's meet tomorrow, if you choose,
Upon the shore, beneath the bridge
That they are building on some endless river
Then he leaves the platform
For the sleeping car that's warm, you realize
He's only advertising one more shelter
And it comes to you, he never was a stranger
And you say, "Ok, the bridge or someplace later."

And then sweeping up the jokers that he left behind
You find he did not leave you very much
Not even laughter
Like any dealer, he was watching for the card that is so high and wild
He'll never need to deal another
He was just some Joseph looking for a manger
He was just some Joseph looking for a manger.

And then leaning on your window sill
He'll say one day you caused his will
To weaken with your love and warmth and shelter
And then taking from his wallet
   an old schedule of trains, he'll say,
"I told you when I came I was a stranger,
I told you when I came I was a stranger."

HEY, THAT'S NO WAY TO SAY GOODBYE

I loved you in the morning
Our kisses sweet and warm
Your hair upon the pillow
Like a sleepy golden storm.
Yes, many loved before us
I know that we are not new
In city and in forest
They smiled like me and you.
But now it's come to distances
And both of us must try

Your eyes are soft with sorrow
Hey, that's no way to say goodbye.

I'm not looking for another
As I wander in my time
Walk me to the corner
Our steps will always rhyme.
You know my love goes with you
As your love stays with me
It's just the way it changes
Like the shoreline and the sea.
But let's not talk of love or chains
And things we can't untie,
Your eyes are soft with sorrow,
Hey, that's no way to say goodbye.

I loved you in the morning
Our kisses deep and warm
Your hair upon the pillow
Like a sleepy golden storm.
Yes, many loved before us
I know that we are not new
In city and in forest
They smiled like me and you.
But let's not talk of love or chains
And things we can't untie,
Your eyes are soft with sorrow
Hey, that's no way to say goodbye.

THE OLD REVOLUTION

I finally broke into prison
I found my place in the chain
Even damnation is poisoned with rainbows
All the brave young men they're waiting now to see a signal
Which some killer will be lighting for pay
   Into this furnace I ask you now to venture
   You whom I cannot betray.

I fought in the old revolution
On the side of the ghost and the king
Of course I was very young and I thought that we were winning
I can't pretend I still feel very much like singing
As they carry the bodies away.
   Into this furnace I ask you now to venture
   You whom I cannot betray.

Lately you've started to stutter
As though you had nothing to say
To all of my architects let me be traitor
Now let me say I myself gave the order
To seek and to search and to destroy.
   Into this furnace I ask you now to venture
   You whom I cannot betray.

You who are broken by power
You who are absent all day
You who are kings for the sake of your children's story
The hand of your beggar is burdened down with money
The hand of your lover is clay.
   Into this furnace I ask you now to venture
   You whom I cannot betray.

PRIESTS

And who will write love songs for you
When I am lord at last
And your body is some little highway shrine
That all my priests have passed
That all my priests have passed.

My priests they will put flowers there
They will stand before the glass
But they'll wear away your little window, love
They will trample on the grass
They will trample on the grass.

And who will shoot the arrow
That men will follow through your grace
When I am lord of memory
And all of your armour has turned to lace
And all your armour has turned to lace?

The simple life of heroes
And the twisted life of saints
They just confuse the sunny calendar
With their red and golden paints
With their red and golden paints.

And all of you have seen the dance
That God has kept from me
But He has seen me watching you
When all your minds were free
When all your minds were free.

(Repeat verses 1 and 2.)

THE STORY OF ISAAC

The door it opened slowly
  My father he came in
  I was nine years old
And he stood so tall above me
  Blue eyes they were shining
  And his voice was very cold.
Said, "I've had a vision
  And you know I'm strong and holy
  I must do what I've been told."
So he started up the mountain
  I was running he was walking
  And his ax was made of gold.

The trees they got much smaller
  The lake a lady's mirror

We stopped to drink some wine
Then he threw the bottle over
  Broke a minute later
  And he put his hand on mine.
Thought I saw an eagle
  But it might have been a vulture,
  I never could decide.
Then my father built an altar
  He looked once behind his shoulder
  He knew I would not hide.

You who build the altars now
  To sacrifice these children
  You must not do it any more.
A scheme is not a vision
  And you never have been tempted
  By a demon or a god.
You who stand above them now
  Your hatchets blunt and bloody,
  You were not there before.
When I lay upon a mountain
  And my father's hand was trembling
  With the beauty of the word.

And if you call me brother now
  Forgive me if I inquire
  Just according to whose plan?
When it all comes down to dust
  I will kill you if I must
  I will help you if I can.
When it all comes down to dust
  I will help you if I must
  I will kill you if I can.
And mercy on our uniform
Man of peace or man of war—
  The peacock spreads his fan.

FROM A LONELY WOODEN TOWER   John Mahoney

Among the sectors of society that have felt the impact of the new poetry, religion has perhaps been most prominent. The whole last decade saw a struggle to apply the goal of relevance to religious institutions. One place some success was quickly found was in the music of religious ceremonies. Originally in the reform, folk music was used; a turn to "new folk" followed shortly afterward.

Consequently, the work of Leonard Cohen is familiar to many who are unaware that he is responsible for "Suzanne." The poem has been heard in churches of every kind. It has formed the musical background for many religiously oriented public programs and even was the theme music of a network special on religion on campus. Many people who learned the poem may have associated it with a recording other than Cohen's own—that of Judy Collins', perhaps; few knew, we could guess, that Leonard Cohen either wrote it or recorded it.

So Leonard Cohen could be at once the best known and the least known of the new poets—"the hyphenates," as Ellen Sanders calls these composer-writer-performers. Even if he is ambivalently recognized, there is some reason to argue that Leonard Cohen is the best.

His work displays how apt it is to ascribe new renaissance virtues to the new poets. Like many 16th-century poets, he makes both the words and the music for his songs. He is particularly fascinated, it seems, by forms and combinations of forms. "The Sisters of Mercy," when examined for visual form, is a four-stanza poem. When it is sung, though, its music provides the overlay of the ballad.

Cohen's work also lends itself—perhaps too easily—to the kind of self-identification that readers of romantic poetry regularly seek. "The Sisters of Mercy," or "Suzanne," may perhaps for this reason be chosen by many other poet-singers who sing not only their own work but that of others whom they admire. They, and those who go away humming the song to themselves, seem less caught by the pretty tune and more ready to be adoptive authors of all that the poems say.

Cohen's collection of works is small. It includes two novels, *The Favorite Game* and *The Beautiful Losers,* and the poems that appear in *Collected Poems, The Leonard Cohen Song Book,* and on his two records. In all these works an autobiographical thread is entirely visible. The temptation to string these threads together in order to talk of "stages" is great, but in the end it is of little help. Two things can be said, however, from studying Leonard Cohen.

For one thing, Leonard Cohen is a poet of religious imagery. He draws from seemingly orthodox Christian sources and from Old Testament Jewish strains alike. For another, his poetry is highly personal, blending the recurring imagery of redemption with a pervading persona. And the "I" of the poem is both poet and reader. The reader benefits from the poem's articulation of the conditions of man, especially today, and its extension of those conditions to the whole heritage of the race.

> You who build these altars now
> To sacrifice these children
> You must not do it anymore.
>> ("The Story of Isaac")

These qualities in his work, however, themselves blend, and can be misleading. Leonard Cohen is a poet of the sacred and of the profane. Poems that are most apparently religious in their imagery are often profane love poems, and simple love poems can be profound in their echo of the history of human religious experience.

A useful oversimplification may be that the perspective of almost all Cohen's poems is *déja vu*. He says again and again that all which seems critical to man has *always* seemed that way. It has all happened before, the sorrows, the emptiness, the betrayals. Such claims are often collective, embracing in the present condition a history of analogues. "The Old Revolution" says, "I finally broke into prison." The entire history of struggle with guilt, morality, and individual sense of right is condensed, in "The Sisters of Mercy," into the epigram:

> When you're not feeling holy
> Your loneliness says that you've sinned.

However, the human instinct to love, to be needed, to depend on another is focused in the lines which, in a sense, conclude from the dominantly religious resonance of "Suzanne":

> [the children] are leaning out for love,
> They will lean that way forever.

If most of the crises of any society have already happened before, if it is all a *déja vu*, in most ages, too, religion articulated these crises and poets reconciled them to life. And if it has been also a particular failure of religion in our own day not to have seen these crises well enough or soon enough to articulate them, it has been a sudden success of poets to have both articulated them and attemped reconciliation.

So these poets' words are speaking for society, whether the quotable line is known for whose it is and what it is, or whether no one seems to hear it at all.

Leonard Cohen's world is one familiar to anyone who has studied poets. The reader of Chaucer can find echoes of Arcite's lament from *The Knight's Tale* in "Hey, That's No Way to Say Goodbye." Both Arcite, as a character, and the speaker in Cohen's poem see at a moment which is final that their loves are "not new," that the world has always offered man that one hope and the same disappointment. Both Chaucer and Cohen see again and again what deserves lamenting in the present world and yearn for a necessary and better one. As poems, both "Priests" and "The Stranger Song" turn on the theme of rejection of innocence and disclaim the presumption of innocence other poets assert.

Cohen seems always, like "many before us," to make the best of human relationships that fight to be original and pristine in the face of the fact that nothing is new, that no one can be original, pristine, or innocent. Yet his work avoids *Weltschmerz*, the Romantic's narcissism that can engulf a poem in autobiography. That characteristic can make a poem admirable, perhaps, but cannot lead the poem to be befriended by its reader or loved for the same reasons.

But Cohen's poems become like words of worship to devotees, their own words, their own thought said in timeless, deliberately ancient images. The Romantic poet says his are the best or worst of times; Cohen says his are archetypal. "The Story of Isaac" can be retold because it is an archetype: somebody has always been having visions of how to satisfy the unknown at the expense of children.

One could in fact suggest that Leonard Cohen is writing liturgies, prayers for the new religions of the time to repeat and to cherish. Whether all the words are clear to the worshipers as they repeat them is no matter. What needs to be articulated is there and understood, and the detail of the articulation of that reality comes clear in the repetition. A subtle criticism of what old religions have done can be heard in "when all your minds were free" from "Priests." The religious imagery suggests this, even if the poem is a love poem. On the other hand, the promise of hope is reaffirmed in "Suzanne"—in its discovery of trust.

In the context of liturgy, Cohen's music is often based on traditional chants. The range, musically, can be remarkably small, the cadences psalmodic and antiphonal. These qualities contribute to the poems' being sung poems. If they seem hard to learn at first, they are easy to sing eventually, and they become obsessive to those who know them.

But while Leonard Cohen is a religious poet by his imagery, in the balance of the sacred with the profane, his greater value lies in his achievement as a poet of lovers.

He seems to take seriously Auden's injunction that "we must love one another or die." And to the student of poets, again, this side of his work is Audenesque. Auden sounds like Cohen at times, comparison shows—or Cohen sounds like Auden:

> With one hand on a hexagram
> And one hand on a girl
> I balance on a wailing wall
> That all men call the world.
> ("Stories of the Street")

Part of his poetry's attractiveness, and part of its worth, is that it corresponds so directly to the reevaluation of love which the new culture has championed. The language he employs is direct, uncloying, and sincere. It celebrates no eternity of the emotion, but it braves the joy of love in the face of its improbability and transient nature:

> Yes, many loved before us
> I know that we are not new
> In city and in forest
> They smiled like me and you
> ("Hey, That's No Way to Say Goodbye")

Even the cynicism, when it appears, is refreshing. Whatever has been given is more than one had a right to expect. It is to be weighed for the better against the host of lesser alternatives that might have been. "The Stranger Song" seems to be the most complete, coherent expression of such a view. The poem combines upbeat, dancing music and prosody with careful narrative poetry of statement.

Even the poems that are clearly antimilitant and antiviolent are turned in phrases of love. Both "The Butcher" and "The Story of Isaac" are dilemmas resolved in their last stanzas by the conciliations that love makes. "The Old Revolution" pleads— and depends on—the promise that love cannot allow betrayal. "Tonight Will Be Fine" will concede to all disadvantages "for a while" for the sake of love.

Though it is a critical trap, finally, to hyperbolize on the present, to make optimistic judgments before history has had its say, the achievement of Leonard Cohen already seems to promise him a place in poetry collections of the future. He seems the best of the new renaissance school of "hyphenates." He is a poet and a composer who applies both crafts to the same artifact with distinctive art. The comparisons of his songs with history, with the troubadours, with Villon, with the lyric poets of the 16th and 17th centuries, with Chaucer and Auden, are natural and easy. He is both an echo, refurbished, of what has been best in the lyric history of poetry and a creative and credible singer for today.

DONOVAN

ATLANTIS

(*Spoken*) The continent of Atlantis was an island which lay before the great flood in the area we now call the Atlantic Ocean. So great an area of land, that from her western shores, those beautiful sailors journeyed to the south and the North Americas with ease, in their ships with painted sails. To the east Africa was a neighbor across a short strait of sea miles. The great Egyptian age is but a remnant of the Atlantian culture.

Hail Atlantis!
Way down below the ocean
Where I wanna be
She may be,
Way down below the ocean

The antedeluvian Kings colonized the world; all the Gods who play in the mythological dramas in all legends from all lands were from fair Atlantis. Knowing her fate, Atlantis sent out ships to all corners of the earth. On board were the twelve, the poet, the physician, the farmer, the scientist, the magician, and the other so-called Gods of our legends. Tho' Gods they were and as the elders of our time choose to remain blind, let us rejoice and let us sing and dance and ring in the new.

Hail Atlantis!
Way down below the ocean
Where I wanna be
She may be,
Way down below the ocean

HURDY GURDY MAN

Thrown like a star in my vast sleep
I opened my eyes to take a peep
To find that I was by the sea
Gazing with tranquility
'Twas then when the Hurdy Gurdy Man
Came singing songs of love
Then when the Hurdy Gurdy Man
Came singing songs of love

Hurdy gurdy hurdy gurdy hurdy gurdy, gurdy he sang
Hurdy gurdy hurdy gurdy hurdy gurdy, gurdy he sang
Hurdy gurdy hurdy gurdy hurdy gurdy, gurdy he sang
Hurdy gurdy hurdy gurdy hurdy gurdy, gurdy he sang
Here comes the roly poly man
And he's singing songs of love
Roly poly roly poly poly roly poly he sang

Histories of ages past
Unenlightened shadows cast
Down through all eternity
The crying of humanity
'Tis then when the Hurdy Gurdy Man
Comes singing songs of love
Then when the Hurdy Gurdy Man
Comes singing songs of love

(Chorus)

THERE IS A MOUNTAIN

The lock upon my garden gate's a snail,
That's what it is.
The lock upon my garden gate's a snail,
That's what it is.

First there is a mountain,
Then there is no mountain,
Then there is.

First there is a mountain,
Then there is no mountain,
Then there is.

The caterpillar sheds his skin

To find a butterfly within.
The caterpillar sheds his skin
To find a butterfly within.

First there is a mountain,
Then there is no mountain,
Then there is.

Oh! Wanita
Oh! Wanita
Oh! Wanita, I call your name.
Oh! The snow will be
A blinding sight to see
As it lies on yonder hillside.

First there is a mountain,
Then there is no mountain,
Then there is.

MELLOW YELLOW

I'm just mad about Saffron,
Saffron's mad about me;
I'm just mad about Saffron,
She's just mad about me.
They call me Mellow Yellow,
(Quite rightly)
They call me Mellow Yellow,
They call me Mellow Yellow,
Born high
Forever to fly,
Wind velocity nil;
Born high
Forever to fly,
If you want your cup I will fill.
They call me Mellow Yellow,
(Quite rightly)
They call me Mellow Yellow,
They call me Mellow Yellow,
He's so mellow, mellow fellow.

Electrical banana
Is gonna be a sudden craze;
Electrical banana
Is bound to be the very next phase;
They call me Mellow Yellow,
They call me Mellow Yellow,
They call me Mellow Yellow, yeah!

I'm just mad about Fourteen,
Fourteen's mad about me;
I'm just mad about Fourteen,
She's just mad about me.
They call me Mellow Yellow,
(Quite rightly)
They call me Mellow Yellow,
They call me Mellow Yellow,
Born high

Forever to fly,
Wind velocity nil;
Born high
Forever to fly,
If you want your cup I will fill.
They call me mellow Yellow,
(Quite rightly)
They call me Mellow Yellow,
They call me Mellow Yellow,
He's so mellow, mellow fellow.

SUNSHINE SUPERMAN

Sunshine came softly
Through my window today,
Could've tripped out easy
But I've changed my ways;
It'll take time, I know it,
But in a while,
You're gonna be mine, I know it,
We'll do it in style,
'Cause I've made my mind up,
You're going to be mine!

I'll tell you right now,
Any trick in the book now, baby,
That I can find,
Everybody's hustlin'
Just to have a little scene,
When I say we'll be cool,
I think that you know what I mean;
We stood at the beach at sunset
Do you remember when?
I know a beach where baby it never ends,
When you've made your mind up

Forever to be mine.
I'll pick up your hand and slowly
Blow your little mind,
Cause I made my mind up,
You're going to be mine.
I'll tell you right now,
Any trick in the book, now, baby,
That I can find.

EPISTLE TO DERROLL

Come all ye starry starfish
living in the deep blue sea
crawl to me i have proposition to make thee
would you walk the north sea floor
to Belgium from England
Bring me word of a banjo man
With a tattoo on his hand.

The spokesman of the starfish
spoke as spokesman should
"If you met our fee then
certainly we would,
If you cast a looking-glass
upon the scallopped sand
You'll have word o' this banjo man
with a tattoo on his hand."

"Come ye starry starfish
I know your ways are caped
maybe its because your astrologically shaped,
Converse with the herring shoals
as I know you can
Bring me word o' the banjo man
with a tattoo on his hand."

The eldest of the starfish
spoke, after a sigh,
"Youthfull as you are young man
you have a 'Wisdom Eye';
Surely you must know a looking-glass
is made from sand?
These youngfish are fooling you
about this banjo man."

"Come then aged starfish
Riddle me no more,
for news I am weary
and my heart is sore;
All on the silent seashore,
help me if you can,
Tell to me if you know
of this banjo man."

"All through the seven oceans
I am a star, most famed,
Many 'leggys' have I lost
and many have I gained,
Strange to say quite recently
I've been to Flemish Land
And if you are courteous
I'll tell you all I can."

"You have my full attention"
I answered him with glee,
His brother stars were twinkling
in the sky above the sea
So I sat there with rapt
attention, on the sand,
very anxious for to hear
of the banjo man.

"I have seen this tattooed hand
through a ship port-hole,
Steaming on the watery main

33 DONOVAN

through the waves so cold,
Heard his tinkling banjo and
his voice so grand
but you must come to Belgium
to shake his tattooed hand."

"Gladly would I come oh
gladly would I go,
Had I not my work to do
and my face to show,
I rejoice to know he's well
but I must go inland,
thank you for the words you brought
of the banjo man."

DONOVAN AS PROPHET Paul D. McGlynn

Trying to analyze Donovan's poetry, we encounter two problems right away. What is innovative in Donovan's lyrics? What is traditional? By now, Richard Goldstein's comment in *The Poetry of Rock* (New York, 1969) that "the great vitality of the pop revolution has been its liberation from . . . encumbrances of form" is well known. Relating Lennon to Joyce, Dylan to Whitman, Donovan to Wordsworth is indeed an empty exercise when critical perception of their music is at stake. Goldstein mentions how, a few years back, Steve Allen played for cheap laughs from the Silent Majority in televisionland by reading pop lyrics out of context, and most of us are familiar with avuncular remarks in and out of classrooms to the same effect: pop music is childish and beneath serious attention. The crux of the problem, of course, is that music has the dimension of existing in space and time—it involves rhythm, harmony, and instrumentation—a dimension that poetry once had itself, no doubt, but one that in this linear age it lacks. The lyrics of modern songs are essentially inseparable from their music.

Nobody should know this better than Steve Allen, himself a musician of some talent, unless it is the archetypal academician who insists on pointing out that, say, "Eleanor Rigby" does not say anything original about lonely people. The Bible, one of our culture's oldest literary sources, points out that there is nothing new under the sun—a trite observation in some peoples' minds—and anyway, we read poetry and listen to music not for the reasons that we read textbooks but because, as Joyce says, we want to perceive as best we can, to enjoy (to dig, if you will) the whatness of the work, its total unique combination of ingredients. This includes, for poetry as well as music, its images, syntax and sound, and rhetoric. For poetry, as for any verbal structure, "rhetoric" means the power of language to effect some response. Music has its own "rhetoric," which can also effect responses; it is the relationship between lyrics and that other dimension, beyond the gravitational pull of words, that includes harmony, rhythm, and instrumentation. Who listens to "Eleanor Rigby" to learn about sociology? Who reads or ever did read *Paradise Lost* to learn about God? Who in his right mind would read Shakespeare's Sonnet 129 to learn about sex?

But if we do decide to analyze Donovan's poetry—that is, his lyrics outside their musical context—then we must disregard Goldstein's injunction in letter, though not in spirit. For it does Donovan's poetic reputation no disservice to link him with the mainstream of poetry in our Western culture. To do so is certainly a compliment, but it is more: I intend, within the framework suggested by my introductory comments, to make a descriptive analysis of Donovan's major themes and images and to suggest some of the poetic directions he seems to be taking.

It seems to me that Donovan is most clearly linked with established poetic tradition by the prophetic quality of much of his work. A prophet, of course, is not one who simply sees the future, but one who sees the present and reads its implications. He can see time not as an hourglass—future on top, present in middle, past on the bottom—but as a continuum constantly perceptible. Donovan often prophesies or speaks of prophetic figures. And though no clear, detailed, and coherent vision has yet emerged, we do have it in a broad sketch.

Perhaps the best known of his prophetic works is "Atlantis," prose to be spoken with a simple musical accompaniment and followed by a sung refrain:

> The continent of Atlantis was an island which lay before the great flood in the area we now call the Atlantic Ocean. So great an area of land, that from her western shores, those beautiful sailors journeyed to the south and the North Americas with ease, in their ships with painted sails. To the east Africa was a neighbor across a short strait of sea miles. The great Egyptian age is but a remnant of the Atlantian culture.

The second prose "stanza" goes:

> The antedeluvian Kings colonized the world; all the Gods who play in the mythological dramas in all legends from all lands were from fair Atlantis. Knowing her fate, Atlantis sent out ships to all corners of the earth. On board were the twelve, the poet, the physician, the farmer, the scientist, the magician, and the other so-called Gods of our legends. Tho' Gods they were and as

the elders of our time choose to remain blind, let us rejoice and let us sing and dance and ring in the new.

The refrain, sung and chanted in a rhapsodic way by a chorus, follows:

Hail Atlantis!
Way down below the ocean
Where I wanna be
She may be,
Way down below the ocean.

The major elements of prophecy are included here, as they have been from Tiresias of Greek mythology to Bob Dylan: modern leaders, "elders," are blind, and present conventions and formalities have to be suspended—through song and dance, for example—to let in the new. Prophecy has always been associated with magic, the occult, ecstasy, or some such nonrational process, because in order truly to commune with truth, the mind has to change gears. If Dylan should sing:

The vagabond who's rapping at your door
Is standing in the clothes that you once wore
            ("It's All Over Now, Baby Blue")

to, say, Attorney General John Mitchell (a pleasant situation that doesn't seem likely to happen), we would have, to borrow Dr. Johnson's metaphor, an owl introduced to day. Nothing will be communicated unless Mr. Mitchell tried, perhaps through the mind-suspending rhythms of electric rock, to see through Dylan's eyes. When Donovan proposes that we "sing and dance and ring in the new," he is suggesting perhaps the only practical program for arriving at a profounder vision than the "elders of our time" will permit themselves.

At this point someone is bound to demand whether this role of prophet is one that Donovan really means to assume for himself. Or is he merely cashing in on the Age of Aquarius with its current fad for the occult? This is an impossible question to answer, and I think it an unfair one. The alternatives are unrealistic. Was Shakespeare "pure," or did he write for money? There are no doubt millions to be made from this sort of music, but the rhetorical posture of prophet (or of anything else) is not in itself *imposture*. I have heard no pacifists or socialists begrudging Joan Baez her earnings, and in fact I suspect most of them enjoy the idea of her making money and forcing the government to hire tax lawyers to get it from her. Nowadays prophets make profits. It's about time. Look what Tiresias and Cassandra got for their pains. Look at Christ. Look at Abraham, Martin, and John. Prophecy is an unpopular pastime, current fads notwithstanding. If Donovan has chosen the role, he has also chosen the contempt of the Silent Majority, who really exist, and who really are shaken up by long hair and beads and ecstatic rhythms, and who really will foreclose on him in some terrible way if provoked enough.

Subversion, in fact, is the fundament of this kind of poetry. "Atlantis" is gay and gentle, qualities common to most of Donovan's work. What is subversive is the anticipation of change. Birth and death are the biggest events in life, each a transition to a wholly unknown state of existence. Perhaps they are interchangeable. The myth of birth (an old state, secure and stable, ends, and a new one, dynamic and frightening, begins) is inherent in prophecy. Present stability, mostly a state of our minds anyway, will not last. Thus, for example, Donovan's "Hurdy Gurdy Man" comes along during "vast sleep," from which the poet awakens "to find that I was by the sea/ Gazing with tranquility," listening to the Hurdy Gurdy Man's "songs of love."

In this song change comes, significantly, during the poet's sleep—a time when his rational mind is appropriately lulled and he is disposed for this experience, whose transcendent nature is represented by the visual infinity of the sea. What is the song?

> Hurdy gurdy hurdy gurdy hurdy gurdy, gurdy he sang.
> Hurdy gurdy hurdy gurdy hurdy gurdy, gurdy he sang.
> Hurdy gurdy hurdy gurdy hurdy gurdy, gurdy he sang.
> Hurdy gurdy hurdy gurdy hurdy gurdy, gurdy he sang.

And later:

> Roly poly roly poly poly roly poly he sang.

It is a chant, and like all chants it is more important for its rhythms than for its syntactic sense; no doubt Steve Allen could have considerable fun with this song. The point of the chant is to effect a feeling of empathy and communion, to draw the listener into the ambience of the experience. The Hurdy Gurdy Man is a psalmist, singing to an unenlightened age:

> Histories of ages past
> Unenlightened shadows cast
> Down through all eternity
> The crying of humanity
> 'Tis then when the Hurdy Gurdy Man
> Comes singing songs of love

This genial dream-vision singer is no doubt a benevolent cousin of Dylan's "Mr. Tambourine Man," a minstrel who arrives during a time of supposed stasis and who promises exciting visions. The main difference between them is that Dylan's prophet seems to peddle ephemeral visions. Is he John the Baptist or the neighborhood pusher? The speaker implores the tambourine man to "take me on a trip/ Upon your magic swirling ship" and to "take me disappearing/ Through the smoke rings of my mind" and to "let me forget about today until tomorrow." Donovan's Hurdy Gurdy Man, on the other hand, sings songs of love that have an almost cosmic intent—to dissolve the shadows of history, to soothe the crying of humanity. His function is closer to that of the child who tells Blake to pipe a song about a lamb, or to Blake's own position as piper.

It is impossible to ignore the influence of drugs on the poetry of rock music; some record jackets even include the warning, amusingly reminiscent of those on cigaret packages, that certain cuts should be audited before public broadcast. Presumably they could be hazardous to an FCC licensee's health. But if there is such a theme in Donovan, it is generally covert. Obviously, drugs can produce visions nearly as exciting as those of a 16th-century ecstatic. But with Donovan the overt subversion of civil law (for example, by endorsing illegal drugs) seems pretty well subordinated to what we can call the philosophical subversion of abandoning the logical world for the visionary one. Thus in "There Is a Mountain,"

> First there is a mountain,
> Then there is no mountain,
> Then there is.
> First there is a mountain,
> Then there is no mountain,
> Then there is.

This is perhaps a psychedelic experience, like the blinding snow and the gate lock that becomes a snail elsewhere in the song. But what is important is the bursting forth of truth in what Joyce called an epiphany and Hopkins an inscape:

> The caterpillar sheds his skin
> To find a butterfly within.

It is a puzzling song, and I would suggest that its meaning lies in its deliberate fragmentation. It is oracular, cryptic, the language of sleep and trance. If there is a controlling idea, it is that some fundamental reality, like a Platonic ideal, lies behind (beyond, within) the specious "reality" that we perceive ordinarily. There *is* a mountain. There *is* a butterfly.

"Epistle to Dippy," with its view through strange crystal spectacles and "all kinds of windows," is also more suggestive or associative than syntactic in its development of ideas. Its milieu is not clear. There are plenty of entrances to the apocalyptic world, however, besides narcotics—alcohol, sleep, hypnosis, music, and intense emotional experiences like love and religious revery—and they probably have been used since the first caveman felt especially good about something or had a dream. "Mellow Yellow" presents a figure remarkably close to Dylan's tambourine man:

> Born high
> Forever to fly,
> Wind velocity nil;
> Born high
> Forever to fly,
> If you want your cup I will fill.

And "Sunshine Superman," who promises to "pick up your hand and slowly/Blow your little mind" is even more overt about the language of drugs.

But this is an ephemeral theme in Donovan. What is central to his poetry is the rhetoric of prophecy. It is the view traditionally presented by prophets: present blindness, a long period of waiting and suffering, a vision (often in a dream or a revived myth, like Atlantis), and a time of Dionysian abandon (singing, dancing, chanting, drinking) to effect the transition. In all this Donovan is inclined less toward the immediate social-political causes than toward the broken home of all mankind. Immediate causes end up as slogans on rear bumpers: "Support our boys—bring them home," "Don't buy California grapes," and the like. He seems to hear, as Arnold and Sophocles heard, the melancholy long withdrawing roar of Faith at low tide. This is what "Atlantis" and "Hurdy Gurdy Man" are apparently concerned with. The exception, of course, is "To Susan on the West Coat Waiting," which as far as I know is the most specifically oriented "protest" poem in his works. Andy in Vietnam tells Susan that like the elders in "Atlantis," "Our fathers have painfully lost their way," but that she should

> Hear me when I say
> There will come a day
> When kings will know
> And love can grow.

Despite the immediacy of this song's concern, the elements we have seen in other works remain: blind fathers, a singer enlightened by love, prophecy of a time of universal enlightenment and love. The message is subversive only for the self-blinded leaders who have split up the family of man and sent it to war against its own.

What is most pervasive in Donovan's work is a paradoxical phenomenon—gentle prophecy. For prophecy by nature is frightening, cataclysmic. When the Atlantian gods come up the Hudson River, who will not run? Who will be awakened by the

Hurdy Gurdy Man and not be alarmed? To see with new spectacles through new windows, to blow your mind—these events are traumatic. Even the metaphysic of Donovan's love-ballad imagery is apocalyptic: he wants to wear his love like heaven; he tells his lover he wants to be "in the warm-hold of your lovin' mind"; freedom is being loved. But Donovan doesn't dwell on the fright. He points to joys, to the wonders beyond our familiar realms, without doom and without the parturient terrors that usually accompany such journeys.

The trip is to the land of metaphor, where all poets and prophets ultimately take us, the land where logic, systems, and all mind-forged manacles are dissolved. Donovan calls it "The Land of Doesn't Have to Be," but Atlantis or dreamland will do. It is a vision a little reminiscent of Cummings or Blake; the harder you try to get there, the less likely that you'll get in. For Blake, the Tigers of Wrath had the ultimate wisdom. For Donovan, the lover-singer has it, and sometimes the child:

> Children fair
> They ride there
> On the dreamy mare.

But at the gate of this metaphoric place, which is surrounded by a "wall of doubt,"

> Waiters wait
> They must fill the form
> Denounce the norm
> They are torn
> 'Twixt praise and scorn.

For the Prufrocks of the world: No Admittance. In short Donovan is a prophet of love. Like Blake, he sings of innocence and of experience, "Little Boy in Corduroy" and "Sunshine Superman." One finds his Atlantis by saving "a sunny wish for a rainy day," and the other takes the more drastic step of blowing his lover's mind. But he is a gentle prophet who respects love and the ways of finding it.

JUDY COLLINS

SINCE YOU'VE ASKED

What I'll give you since you asked
Is all my time together
Take the rugged sunny days
The warm and Rocky weather
Take the roads that I have walked along
Looking for tomorrow's time
Peace of mind.

As my life spills into yours
Changing with the hours

Filling up the world with time
Turning time to flowers
I can show you all the songs
That I never sang to one man before.

We have seen a million stones lying by the water
You have climbed the hills with me to the mountain shelter
Taken off the days one by one
Setting them to breathe in the sun.

Take the lilies and the lace
From the days of childhood
All the willow winding paths
Leading up and outward
This is what I give
This is what I ask you for
Nothing more.

MY FATHER

My father always promised us
   that we would live in France,
We'd go boating on the Seine
   and I would learn to dance.
We lived in Ohio then
   he worked in the mines,
On his streams like boats we knew
   we'd sail, in time.

All my sisters soon were gone
   to Denver and Cheyenne,
Marrying their grownup dreams,
   the lilacs and the man.
I stayed behind the youngest still,
   only danced alone,

The colors of my father's dreams
   faded without a sound.

And I live in Paris now,
   my children dance and dream
Hearing the ways of a miner's life
   in words they've never seen.
I sail my memories of home
   like boats across the Seine,
And watch the Paris sun
   set in my father's eyes again.

My father always promised us
   that we would live in France,
We'd go boating on the Seine
   and I would learn to dance.
We lived in Ohio then
   he worked in the mines,
On his streams like boats we knew
   we'd sail, in time.

ALBATROSS

The lady comes to the gate
Dressed in lavender and leather
Looking North to the sea
She finds the weather fine
She hears the steeple bells
Ringing through the orchard all the way from town
She watches seagulls fly
Silver on the ocean
Stitching through the waves the edges of the sky
Many people wander up the hills from all around you
Making up your memories and thinking they have found you
They cover you with veils of wonder

As if you were a bride
Young men holding violets are curious to know
If you have cried
And tell you why and ask you why
Either way you answer
Lace around the collars
Of the blouses of the ladies
Flowers from a Spanish friend
Of the family
The embroidery of your life
Holds you in and keeps you out
But you survive
Imprisoned in your bones
Behind the isinglass windows of your eyes.
And in the night the iron wheels
   rolling through the rain
Down the hills through the long grass
   to the sea,
And in the dark the hard bells
   ringing with pain
Come away alone

Even now by the gate
With your long hair blowing,
And the colors of the day
That lie along your arms,
You must barter your life
To make sure you are living,
And the crowd that has come,
You give them the colors,
And the bells and the wind and the dreams.
Will there never be a prince
Who rides along the sea and the mountains,
Scattering the sand and foam
Into amethyst fountains,
Riding up the hills from the beach
In the long summer grass,
Holding the sun in his hands
And shattering the isinglass?

Day and night and day again,
And people come and go away forever,
While the shining summer sea
Dances in the glass of your mirror,
While you search the waves for love
And your visions for a sign,
The knot of tears around your throat
Is crystalizing into your design.
And in the night the iron wheels
    rolling through the rain
Down the hills through the long grass
    to the sea,
And in the dark the hard bells
    ringing with pain,
Come away alone
Come away alone . . . with me.

TED JOANS

IN HOMAGE TO HEAVY LOADED TRANE, J.C.

J.C. in these
sentences of three
read by
Stokely C. Allen G. & me
London summer '67
J.C. it said:
sheets of sound
           MASCULINE MUSCLE MOODS OF BLUES
S   e   r   p
        e
          n
           t
          i
           n e screams of happiness

hot molted masses of marvelous messages
and HEAVY anger
                    p
                     o
                      u
                       r
                        i
                         n
                          g
              forth from fiery throats
of your thick reeds
spurting rhythms
all over
all under
and all around
J.C.
Mr. Trane
J.C.
John Coltrane
with pain
we read
three short English lines
of your dying
and we strain
J.C.
black people & me
to keep
from crying

DON L. LEE

ASSASSINATION

it was wild.
the
bullet hit high.
                (the throat-neck)
& from everywhere,
     the motel, from under bushes and cars,
     from around corners and across streets,
     out of the garbage cans and from rat holes
     in the earth
they came running.
with
guns

        drawn
        they came running
    toward the King—
                    all of them
                    fast and sure—
        as if
        the King
        was going to fire back.
        they came running,
        fast and sure,
        in the
        wrong
        direction.

BUT HE WAS COOL
OR: HE EVEN STOPPED FOR GREEN LIGHTS

super-cool
ultrablack
a tan/purple
had a beautiful shade.

he had a double-natural
that wd put the sisters to shame.
his dashikis were tailor made
& his beads were imported sea shells
    (from some blk/country i never heard of)
he was triple-hip.

his tikis were hand carved
out of ivory
& came express from the motherland.
he would greet u in swahili
& say good-by in yoruba.
woooooooooooo-jim he bes so cool & ill tel li gent
            cool-cool is so cool he was un-cooled by other niggers' cool

cool-cool ultracool was bop-cool/ice box cool so cool cold cool
his wine didn't have to be cooled, him was air conditioned cool
cool-cool/real cool made me cool—now ain't that cool
cool-cool so cool him nick-named refrigerator.

cool-cool so cool
he didn't know,
after detroit, newark, chicago &c.,
we had to hip
          cool-cool/ super-cool/ real cool
     that
to be black
is
to be
very-hot.

JOHN LENNON-PAUL McCARTNEY

BLACKBIRD

Blackbird singing in the dead of night
Take these broken wings and learn to fly
All your life
You were only waiting for this moment to arise.

Blackbird singing in the dead of night
Take these sunken eyes and learn to see
All your life
You were only waiting for this moment to be free.

Blackbird fly   Blackbird fly
Into the light of the dark black night.

Blackbird fly   Blackbird fly
Into the light of the dark black night.

Blackbird singing in the dead of night
Take these broken wings and learn to fly
All your life
You were only waiting for this moment to arise
You were only waiting for this moment to arise
You were only waiting for this moment to arise.

THE CONTINUING STORY OF BUNGALOW BILL

Hey, Bungalow Bill
What did you kill
Bungalow Bill?

He went out tiger hunting with his elephant and gun
In case of accidents he always took his mom
He's the all American bullet-headed saxon mother's son.
All the children sing

Hey, Bungalow Bill
What did you kill
Bungalow Bill?

Deep in the jungle where the mighty tiger lies
Bill and his elephants were taken by surprise
So Captain Marvel zapped in right between the eyes
All the children sing

Hey, Bungalow Bill
What did you kill
Bungalow Bill?

The children asked him if to kill was not a sin
Not when he looked so fierce, his mother butted in
If looks could kill it would have been us instead of him
All the children sing

Hey, Bungalow Bill
What did you kill
Bungalow Bill?

HAPPINESS IS A WARM GUN

She's not a girl who misses much
Do do do do do do do do
She's well acquainted with the touch of the velvet hand
Like a lizard on a window pane.

The man in the crowd with the multicoloured mirrors
On his hobnail boots
Lying with his eyes while his hands are busy
  Working overtime
A soap impression of his wife which he ate
And donated to the National Trust.

I need a fix 'cause I'm going down
Down to the bits that I left uptown
I need a fix 'cause I'm going down
Mother Superior jump the gun
Mother Superior jump the gun
Mother Superior jump the gun
Mother Superior jump the gun.

Happiness is a warm gun
Happiness is a warm gun
When I hold you in my arms
And I feel my finger on your trigger
I know no one can do me no harm
Because happiness is a warm gun
  —Yes it is.

MAXWELL'S SILVER HAMMER

Joan was quizzical
Studied metaphysical science in the home
Late night all alone with a test tube oh oh oh oh

Maxwell Edison
Majoring in medicine calls her on the phone
Can I take you out to the pictures Jo-o-o-oan

As she's getting ready to go
A knock comes on the door
Bang bang Maxwell's silver hammer
Came down on her head
Bang bang Maxwell's silver hammer
Made sure she was dead

Back in school again
Maxwell plays the fool again, teacher gets annoyed
Wishing to avoid an unpleasant sce-e-e-ene

She tells Max to stay
When the class is gone away and he waits behind
Writing fifty times "I must not be so-o-o-o-"

But when she turns her back on the boy
He creeps up from behind
Bang bang Maxwell's silver hammer
Came down on her head
Bang bang Maxwell's silver hammer
Made sure she was dead

PC thirty-one
Said we caught a dirty one, Maxwell stands alone
Painting testimonial pictures oh oh oh oh

Rose and Valerie
Screaming from the gallery say he must go free
The judge does not agree and he tells them so-o-o-o

But as the words are leaving his lips

A noise comes from behind
Bang bang Maxwell's silver hammer
Comes down on his head
Bang bang Maxwell's silver hammer
Made sure he was dead

Sil-ver ham-mer oh

JONI MITCHELL

MICHAEL FROM MOUNTAINS

Michael wakes you up with sweets
He takes you up streets and the rain comes down
Sidewalk markets locked up tight
And umbrellas bright on a grey background
There's oil on the puddles in taffeta patterns
That run down the drain
In colored arrangements
That Michael will change with a stick that he found

Chorus:
Michael from mountains
Go where you will go to

Know that I will know you
Someday I may know you very well

Michael brings you to a park
He sings and it's dark when the clouds come by
Yellow slickers up on swings
Like puppets on strings hanging in the sky
They'll splash home to suppers in wallpapered kitchens
Their mothers will scold
But Michael will hold you
To keep away cold till the sidewalks are dry—

(Chorus)

Michael leads you up the stairs
He needs you to care and you know you do
Cats come crying to the key
And dry you will be in a towel or two
There's rain in the window
There's sun in the painting that smiles on the wall
You want to know all
But his mountains have called so you never do—

(Chorus)

CHELSEA MORNING

Woke up, it was a Chelsea morning, and the first thing that I heard
Was a song outside my window, and the traffic wrote the words
It came ringing up like Christmas bells, and rapping up like pipes and drums

Oh, won't you stay
We'll put on the day
And we'll wear it 'till the night comes

Woke up, it was a Chelsea morning, and the first thing that I saw
Was the sun through yellow curtains, and a rainbow on the wall
Red, green and gold welcome you, crimson crystal beads to beckon

Oh, won't you stay
We'll put on the day
There's a sun show every second

Now the curtain opens on a portrait of today
And the streets are paved with passersby
And pigeons fly
And papers lie
Waiting to blow away

Woke up, it was a Chelsea morning, and the first thing that I knew
There was milk and toast and honey and a bowl of oranges, too
And the sun poured in like butterscotch and stuck to all my senses

Oh, won't you stay
We'll put on the day
And we'll talk in present tenses

When the curtain closes and the rainbow runs away
I will bring you incense owls by night
By candlelight
By jewel-light
If only you will stay
Pretty baby, won't you
Woke up, it is a Chelsea morning

BOTH SIDES, NOW

Rows and flows of angel hair
And ice cream castles in the air
And feather canyons ev'rywhere
I've looked at clouds that way

But now they only block the sun
They rain and snow on ev'ryone
So many things I would have done
But clouds got in my way

I've looked at clouds from both sides now
From up and down, and still somehow
It's cloud illusions I recall
I really don't know clouds at all

Moons and Junes and Ferris wheels
The dizzy dancing way you feel
As ev'ry fairy tale comes real
I've looked at love that way

But now it's just another show
You leave 'em laughing when you go
And if you care, don't let them know
Don't give yourself away

I've looked at love from both sides now
From give and take, and still somehow
It's love's illusions I recall
I really don't know love at all

Tears and fears and feeling proud
To say "I love you" right out loud
Dreams and schemes and circus crowds
I've looked at life that way

But now old friends are acting strange
They shake their heads, they say I've changed
But something's lost, but something's gained
In living ev'ry day

I've looked at life from both sides now
From win and lose and still somehow
It's life's illusions I recall
I really don't know life at all

I've looked at life from both sides now
From up and down, and still somehow
It's life's illusions I recall
I really don't know life at all

MARCIE

Marcie in a coat of flowers
Stops inside a candy store
Reds are sweet and greens are sour
Still no letter at her door
So she'll wash her flower curtains
Hang them in the wind to dry
Dust her tables with his shirt and
Wave another day goodbye

Marcie's faucet needs a plumber
Marcie's sorrow needs a man
Red is autumn green is summer
Greens are turning and the sand
All along the ocean beaches
Stares up empty at the sky
Marcie buys a bag of peaches
Stops a postman passing by
And summer goes
Falls to the sidewalk like string and brown paper
Winter blows
Up from the river there's no one to take her
To the sea

Marcie dresses warm, it's snowing
Takes a yellow cab uptown
Red is stop and green's for going
Sees a show and rides back down
Down along the Hudson River
Past the shipyards in the cold
Still no letter's been delivered
Still the winter days unfold
Like magazines
Fading in dusty grey attics and cellars
Make a dream
Dream back to summer and hear how he tells her
Wait for me

Marcie leaves and doesn't tell us
Where or why she moved away

Red is angry green is jealous
That was all she had to say
Someone thought they saw her Sunday
Window shopping in the rain
Someone heard she bought a one-way ticket
And went west again.

SONGS TO AGING CHILDREN COME

Through the windless wells of wonder
By the throbbing light machine
In a tea leaf trance or under
Orders from the king and queen

Songs to aging children come
Aging children, I am one

People hurry by so quickly
Don't they hear the melodies
In the chiming and the clicking
And the laughing harmonies

Songs to aging children come
Aging children, I am one

Some come dark and strange like dying
Crows and ravens whistling
Lines of weeping, strings of crying
So much said in listening

Songs to aging children come
Aging children, I am one

Does the moon play only silver
When it strums the galaxy
Dying roses will they will their
Perfumed rhapsodies to me

Songs to aging children come
This is one

63   JONI MITCHELL

SONGS OF AN AGING CHILD   John Schmittroth

As performer, Joni Mitchell, a pretty, long-legged, long-haired blonde, seems a Modigliani, a little girl in braids grown suddenly almost wise through sadness. Wistful and ingenuous, she sings alone at stage center accompanying herself on guitar or piano. On her popular albums, through electronic dubbing, her own voice is a sensitive accompanying instrument.

In her late twenties Canada-born Joni is successful as composer and as interpreter of her own music. Her songs are included in the repertoires of several other "new folk" artists, most notably that of her good friend Judy Collins, who has built a part of her own career on "Michael from Mountains," "Winter Grey," and "Both Sides, Now."

And the stunning album cover art, which offers another medium's insights into her subjects, themes, and tones, is of her own design.

Each of these talents—composer, musician, designer—contributes to another skill as yet unrecognized: the song lyrics of Joni Mitchell mark her as a promising young poet.

A woman holding an exotic bird dominates the lush, delicately drawn face of her first album. Long, intricately patterned hair threaded with delicate flowers falls down her back. On her head is a black and gray silk Juliet cap decorated with pearls. At the very top a delicate glass bauble holds a photograph. On the left and above, setting off the figure, are large, tropical flowers; on the right, a flight of seagulls, a setting sun, and a pirate ship. Watercolor oranges, yellows, and greens dominate the montage.

The center of the back cover is a blowup of the inset photograph. It shows Miss Mitchell with orange transparent umbrella, a suitcase, and a guitar standing in the rain next to a small van in a littered city street. Enchanting Beardsleyesque small creatures and plants frame the picture. At lower left a peacock stares at the girl; at upper right are cactus trees; at lower right are large flowers in delicate pastels. Again greens, browns, and shades of orange predominate.

This richness of color and intricacy of design indicate a unique feminine consciousness whose milieu is a blending of reality and fairytale wonder.

Most of Miss Mitchell's poems, too, are centered on a young woman in her twenties who sees the world, much as an older Alice might, as a potpourri, usually sad, of real and imagined flowers.

Through the poems runs a single pastel story of the few successes and many failures of a girl searching for love. She once "had a king in a tenement castle/ Lately he's taken to painting the pastel walls brown/ He's taken the curtains down":

I had a king dressed in drip-dry and paisley
Lately he's taken to saying I'm crazy and blind

Finally, she is abandoned, a queen in the grove. "The King's on the road."

She is rescued by "Michael from Mountains," who can transform with his magic the ugliness of rain in the city to "the sun in the painting that smiles from the wall." He, too, though, may stay only a short time and must leave when his mountains call. There is evidence for reading this poem allegorically, making Michael a symbol of the rich inner life capable of transmuting base reality. With only "a stick that he found," for example, Michael can change the "colored arrangements" of an oil slick on a rain-soaked pavement. And the chorus, repeated three times, vows that someday the speaker will get to know Michael very well.

The city, whose ugliness Michael transcends, can be wondrous and exciting. "There are places to come from and places to go." But more frequently "You feed it all your woes." It's a nightmare, "a ghostly garden/ With gangs and girlie shows." (In "Nathan La Franeer" there are three such grotesque parodies of the nursery-rhyme Mary's garden.)

The city usually is a place to flee—to the simplicity and pastoral charm of the country, to "Sisotowbell Lane," where

Jovial neighbors come down when they will
With stories to tell

and where there are "muffin buns and berries/By the steamy kitchen window," and a rocking chair and stars and "a candle in the window."

Most frequently, the country is a seascape with "peridots and periwinkle blue medallions," where "Mermaids live in colonies," where one can share his dreams with the seagull, symbol of freedom.

The sea, however, may betray you, too. It may bring someone you thought a prince, who once brought gifts of "silks and sandalwood and Persian lace," who turns out to be a pirate who'll "sink you with a kiss" and "steal your heart and sail away."

In city or country, at the seaside or in a yellow-slickered neighborhood park in the rain, there are days when the world is beautiful. There are "Chelsea Mornings" with "milk and toast and honey and a bowl of oranges, too," when "the sun poured in like butterscotch and stuck to all my senses," a day you can "put on," with "a sun show every second." There are days, especially after one has stayed up all night, when morning "comes up like a dream/ All muted and misty." And by love this world is taught to sing. Life is meeting a man in a Bleecker street café with "sorrow in his eyes," or at the seashore "a golden Prince," or on the midway one who stands out "like a ruby in a black man's ear." All are "Songs to Aging Children Come," in a magical, musical garden. A few songs chime and click and have "laughing harmonies." But

> Some come dark and strange like dying
> Crows and ravens whistling
> Lines of weeping, strings of crying.

One of the best of these songs, one of the most fully realized poems, is "Marcie." As usual, the poem is hung on a slight, sad narrative. Marcie has been asked to wait by a boy who left her. She does—for a year of growing anxiety and despair. Finally, angry and jealous, "she bought a one-way ticket/ And went west again." The skill of the song is in its conciseness, in its unifying symbolism, and most of all in its imagery. And all is carried off with a musician's ear for rhythm and a painter's eye for detail. The first four lines tell the story with remarkable economy:

> Marcie in a coat of flowers
> Stops inside a candy story
> Reds are sweet and greens are sour
> Still no letter at her door

Immediately one realizes sadly that she has, in Jessamyn West's phrase, "the scent of the victim," that her innocence has betrayed her. So there is dramatic irony in watching her washing curtains, dusting with his shirt; in seeing spring slowly turn to summer, summer's green becoming autumn's red, and finally winter blowing in.

As Marcie's story unfolds, pathos grows. She "buys a bag of peaches"; each day she "stops a postman going by"; she "takes a yellow cab uptown"; "Sees a show and rides back down"; window shops alone in the rain. Overall there is a dreamlike quality as story turns to poem and poem to poem-in-slow-motion. Before your eyes the vivid images congeal to symbols. Red and green candies, reds of autumn and greens of summer, red and green stop signals, and the red of anger and green of jealousy, in becoming a symbolic structure, unify the poem almost like a refrain.

Marcie is finally an aging child to whom a sad song has come. And Joni Mitchell herself is an aging prodigy. She is extraordinarily skillful in the music of language— its rhyming and its rhythms. She has a poet's hunger for words and a painter's deft skill with images. And most important she has a unique sensibility capable of creating "both sides" of a small, poignant world—its illusions and its realities.

LAURA NYRO

HANDS OFF THE MAN (FLIM FLAM MAN)

Hands off the man
the flim flam man
his mind is up his sleeve
and his talk is make believe
Oh lord
the man's a fraud
he's a flim flam man

Hands off the man
the flim flam man
he's the one in the Trojan horse

making out like he's Santa Claus
Oh lord
the man's a fraud
he's a flim flam man

everybody wants him
the people and the Police
and all the pretty ladies disarm
the beautiful gent
you know he has hardly a cent
he pays his monthly rent
with daily charm

Hands off the man
the flim flam man
his mind is up his sleeve
and his talk is make believe
Oh Lord
the man's a fraud
he's a flim flam man

He's an artist
He's a flim flam man
he's so cagey
he's a flim flam man
he's a fox
he's a flim flam man
don't believe him
he's a flim flam
ole road runner

BUY AND SELL

Cocaine and quiet beers
sweet candy and caramel
pass the time and dry the tears
on a street called buy and sell

Life turns like the endless sea
death tolls like a vesper bell
children laugh and lovers dream
on a street called buy and sell

Ladies dress calico style
beware your heart
when they smile
and their men walk shamelessly
aimlessly by
cinders in the daylight
junkyards in the sky

buy and sell
sell my goods to buy my roof
my bed

Two pennies will buy a rose
three pennies and who can tell?
on a street
that comes and goes
by the name of buy and sell

Sell my goods to buy my roof
my bed

AND WHEN I DIE

I'm not scared of dyin
and I don't really care
if it's peace you find in dyin
well then let the time be near
if it's peace you find in dyin
when the dyin time is here
just bundle up my coffin
cause it's cold way down there
And when I die
and when I'm gone

there'll be one child born
and a world to carry on

My troubles are many
they're as deep as a well
I swear there ain't no heaven
and I pray there ain't no hell
swear there ain't no heaven
and pray there ain't no hell
but I'll never know by livin
only my dyin will tell
And when I die
and when I'm gone
there'll be one child born
and a world to carry on

Give me my freedom
for as long as I be
all I ask of livin
is to have no chains on me
all I ask of livin
and all I ask of dyin
is to go naturally

don't wanna go by the devil
don't wanna go by the demon
don't wanna go by Satan
don't wanna die uneasy
just let me go naturally
And when I die
and when I'm gone
there'll be one child born
and a world to carry on

SAVE THE COUNTRY

Come on people
come on children
come on down to the glory river

gonna wash you up
and wash you down
gonna lay the devil down
Come on people
come on children
there's a king at the glory river
and the precious king
he loved the people to sing
babes in the blinkin' sun
sang we shall overcome!
Come on people sons and mothers
Keep the dream
of the two young brothers
gonna take the dream
and ride the dove
we could build the dream with love
I got fury in my soul
fury's gonna take me to the glory goal
in my mind I can't study war no more
save the people
save the children
save the country

SWEET LOVIN BABY

I belong
to the man
don't belong without him
when I sleep without him
loneliness
loneliness
my dreams with God
softly waiting
I belong to the man

Sweet lovin baby
oh sweet lovin baby

I want you
I could almost die
he says
There's gold in you darling
drew gold
when I woke her
she's an ole chain smoker
Grace
and the Preacher
blown fleets of sweet eyed dreams
tonight

loneliness
loneliness
natural windmill
wheel weave and bless
my bed
my bed
my man

That's lovin baby
Oh sweet lovin baby
where is the night luster?

past my trials

sparkling in flight
in your arms
for all of my life

CAPTAIN SAINT LUCIFER

Mama mama
you're a whiz and a scholar too
mama open up the room lock
sip sip
I'm going to the moon dock
he gives to me

buckles off shingles
off a cockleshell on norway basin
coke and tuna
boots and roses from Russia

Now I'll live and die and rise
with my captain
mama say go

Meet me captain Saint Lucifer
darling I'll be there
don't you know
now don't you know I love you?

Meet me captain Saint Lucifer
la la la la la la la la
oo I love you
Love you I do

Mama mama
you're a whiz and a scholar too
mama I'm at anchor in your glow now
sip sip
even as I go now
he gives to me

buckles off shingles
and a jangle from a congo love chase
early bloomers
made of earth and love lace

Now I'll live and die and rise
with my captain
mama be happy

Meet me captain Saint lucifer
darling I'll be there
don't you know
Meet me captain Saint lucifer
darling I'll be there
don't you know

Gutters in stacks
is where I come from
buckles off a poverty drum
Oh my love trumpet soul
Tell Gabriel
to tell the captain

Thank you baby
you're my baby now

THE CONFESSION

Super summer sugar coppin
in the morning
do your shoppin baby
love my lovething
super ride inside my lovething
you may disappear
but you'll be back I swear
would you love
to love me baby
I would love
to love you baby now
would you love
to love me baby
I would love
to love you baby now
Mama it's my pain
Super summer sugar coppin
in the morning
do your shoppin baby
love my lovething
super ride inside my lovething
You may leave the fair
but you'll be back I swear
would you love
to love me baby

I would love
to love you baby now
would you love
to love me baby
I would love
to love you baby now
I keep hearin
mother cryin
I keep hearin
daddy thru his grave
"little girl
of all the daughters
you were born a woman
not a slave"
Oh I hate my winsome lover
Tell him I've had others
at my breast
but tell him he has held my heart
and only now am I a virgin
I confess

love my lovething
Love is surely gospel

STONED SOUL PICNIC

Can you surry
can you picnic?
Can you surry
Can you picnic?
Surry down
to a stoned soul picnic
Surry down
to a stoned soul picnic
There'll be lots of time and wine
red yellow honey
sassafras and moonshine

Red yellow honey sassafras and moonshine
Stoned soul

Surry down
to a stoned soul picnic
Surry down
to a stoned soul picnic
Rain and sun come in akin
and from the sky come the Lord
and the lightnin
And from the sky come the Lord and the lightnin
Stoned soul

surry surry surry surry
There'll be trains of blossoms
There'll be trains of music
There'll be trains of trust
trains of golden dust
Come along and surry on sweet trains of thought—
surry on down
Can you surry?

Surry down
to a stoned soul picnic
Surry down
to a stoned soul picnic
There'll be lots of time and wine
red yellow honey
sassafras and moonshine
red yellow honey
Sassafras
and moonshine moonshine
Stoned soul
surry surry surry surry
surry surry surry
surry surry
surry—

WRAPPED IN VELVET   Norman McKendrick

Laura Nyro sings from velvet shadows, even when she sings of joy and the beat is insistently happy. She has something to say, something to attend to. She is a little girl dressed up in her mother's clothes and her language is poetry.

Her song is love, a love that is childish and girlish, made up of need and loneliness. Her love comes in the end to the pain of incompatibles: god in a world; god in a man, god in all, in everything. But where is it found? On a trip. In love. In ups and downs. Can you hold it?

Can you be free and possessed, loved and not dominated? What kind of a man is wanted? A flim flam man? He's a flim flam, pays his way with his charm, but it is only daily charm. The song is also entitled "Hands Off the Man." You can't hold on to him. No one minds him, no one could be angry with him. He's even kind of nice. But it's all tinsel and that's cool, but only tinsel and that tends to fizzle, to get tired, you wake up and—blah!

So the street, the city. Sometimes it's a street called buy and sell. You're a commodity, too. You need to sell for survival, for a roof, for a bed. What difference does it make what you sell, or what you use? It's all the same; on this street you can buy cocaine, quiet beers, sweet candy, caramel. It is really the great American principle: If you love me, give me money. There is even a bitter irony in the beauty since two pennies will buy a rose.

So, what the hell, I'm not scared of dyin'. Just let there be no chains—let me be free. That's what the words say, but not really. The same dichotomy is still there: to be held, to be possessed, to be loved, even to be loved in a holy way: "love my lovething/ Love is surely gospel."

She shows us a grownup side in *New York Tendaberry*; she gets bitter. "Save the country" progresses through references to nonviolence, through Martin Luther King, Jr., and religious motivation, through the Kennedy brothers and a new world with love, and ends with no answer at all, no theory, just a simple plea: Save the people, save the children, save the country.

I'm sure she would be surprised to hear it called this, but her theology gets tough, too. She sings that she belongs to the man: "don't belong without him/ when I sleep without him/ loneliness." Once again, despite all the claims for freedom, there is the need for permanence, for fulfillment, for totality, and the otherness that involves. Can God be the other? "My dreams with God/ softly waiting/ I belong to the man." Why? Because only the man can find the gold in her—can draw it from her— only then will she pass her trials and discover herself the star she is: "sparkling in flight/ in your arms/ for all of my life." And we are back to "love my love-thing/ Love is surely gospel."

She gropes, really she claws at an answer. To find your love in god, to hide in a womb god, a mama god, is wrong, is to be bound, is to die, is to fail to mine the gold, to fail to realize and reveal the god in yourself, which is the only real god available to you.

But how do you combine the need to love, to love and be loved, to be possessed, to be permanent, to be holy—Captain Saint Lucifer? The answer is in the title. He is a captain: the lover will dominate, will possess. He is a saint: he will be holy—he will relate and reveal—will not be flim flam—will, in fact, be god. He is Lucifer: but he will be evil too, evil in the square sense—this won't be an antiseptic love. So she's "going to the moon dock/ he gives to me." And a whole world of noncity, nonbuy-and-sell imagery explodes and is contrasted with the imagery of the city and religion. The combination sought is found and expressed in the religious and erotic lines: "Now I'll live and die and rise/ with my captain/ mama say go." And she has her answer—if she can find such a combination in the world we all live in.

We hear in her the cry of lovers, of poets, of saints since anyone started to care. She resisted, I think, but in the end is a woman.

Much more could be said, but this is the core: the child in the woman needing, wanting, fearing, hiding, revealing, exulting, seeking, and always saying and always begging: love me. And she is perfectly correct: love is surely gospel.

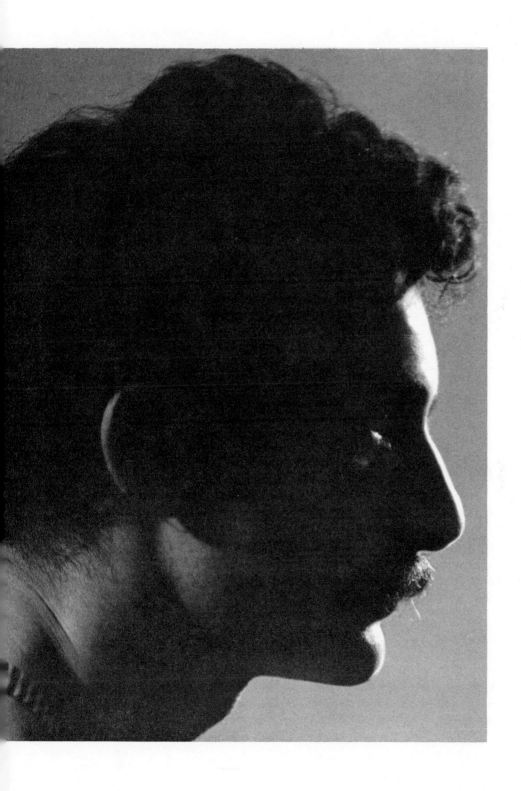

PHIL OCHS

CRUCIFIXION

And the night comes again to the circle-studded sky,
The stars settle slowly, in loneliness they lie.
Till the universe explodes as a falling star is raised;
The planets are paralyzed, the mountains are amazed;
But they all glow brighter from the brilliance of the blaze;
With the speed of insanity, then, he dies!

In the green fields of turning, a baby is born;
His cries crease the wind, and mingle with the morn;
An assault upon the order, the changing of the guard;
Chosen for a challenge that's hopelessly hard;
And the only single sign is the sighing of the stars;
But to the silence of distance they're sworn!

So dance, dance, dance
Teach us to be true;
Come dance, dance, dance;
'Cause we love you.

Images of innocence charge him to go on
But the decadence of history is looking for a pawn
To a nightmare of knowledge he opens up the gate
A blinding revelation is served upon his plate
That beneath the greatest love is a hurricane of hate
And God help the critic of the dawn.

So he stands on the sea and he shouts to the shore
But the louder that he screams the longer he's ignored
For the wine of oblivion is drunk to the dregs
And the merchants of the masses almost have to be begged
Till the giant is aware that someone's pulling at his leg
And someone is tapping at the door.

So dance, dance, dance
Teach us to be true;
Come dance, dance, dance;
'Cause we love you.

Then his message gathers meaning and it spreads across the land
The rewarding of the fame is the following of the man
But ignorance is everywhere and people have their way
And success is an enemy to the losers of the day
In the shadows of the churches who knows what they pray
And blood is the language of the band.

The Spanish bulls are beaten, the crowd is soon beguiled
The matador is beautiful, a symphony of style
Excitement is ecstatic, passion places bets,
Gracefully he bows to ovations that he gets
But the hands that are applauding are slippery with sweat
And saliva is falling from their smiles.

So dance, dance, dance
Teach us to be true;
Come dance, dance, dance;
'Cause we love you.

Then this overflow of life is crushed into a liar
The gentle soul is ripped apart and tossed in to the fire
It's the burial of beauty, it's the victory of night.
Truth becomes a tragedy limping from the light
The heavens are horrified, they stagger from the sight
And the cross is trembling with desire.

They say they can't believe it, it's a sacrilegious shame
Now who would want to hurt such a hero of the game
But you know I predicted it I knew he had to fall
How did it happen, I hope his suffering was small
Tell me every detail I've got to know it all
And do you have a picture of the pain.

So dance, dance, dance
Teach us to be true;
Come dance, dance, dance;
'Cause we love you.

Time takes her toll and the memory fades
But his glory is growing in the magic that he made
Reality is ruined there is nothing more to fear
The drama is distorted to what they want to hear
Swimming in their sorrow in the twisting of a tear
As they wait for the new thrill parade.

The eyes of the rebel have been branded by the blind
To the safety of sterility the threat has been refined
The child was created to the slaughter house he's led
So good to be alive when the eulogies are read
The climax of emotion the worship of the dead
As the cycle of sacrifice unwinds.

So dance, dance, dance
Teach us to be true;
Come dance, dance, dance;
'Cause we love you.

And the night comes again to the circle-studded sky,
The stars settle slowly, in loneliness they lie.

Till the universe explodes as a falling star is raised;
The planets are paralyzed, the mountains are amazed;
But they all glow brighter from the brilliance of the blaze;
With the speed of insanity, then, he dies!

BUFFY SAINTE-MARIE

MAPLE SUGAR BOY

Maple sugar boy
Maple sugar brown
Lying in the sun
and getting browner

Sad little girl
Sad little tear
Never felt more helpless
Never downer

Bad little boy
Lonely little girl
Lonely little heart
Filled up with tears

This little love
Lasted but a kiss
One that I'll remember
Through the years

UNTIL IT'S TIME FOR YOU TO GO

You're not a dream, you're not an angel
You're a man
I'm not a queen, I'm a woman
Take my hand
We'll make a space in the lives
That we'd planned
And here we'll stay
Until it's time for you to go

Yes we're different, worlds apart
We're not the same
We laughed and played at the start
Like in a game
You could have stayed outside my heart
But in you came
And here we'll stay
Until it's time for you to go

Don't ask why
Don't ask how
Don't ask forever
Love me now

This love of mine had no beginning
It has no end
I was an oak, now I'm a willow
Now I can bend
And though I'll never in my life
See you again
Here we'll stay
Until it's time for you to go

Don't ask why of me
Don't ask how of me
Don't ask forever of me
Love me, love me now

You're not a dream, you're not an angel
You're a man
I'm not a queen, I'm a woman
Take my hand
We'll make a space in the lives
That we'd planned
And here we'll stay
Until it's time for you to go

PAUL SIMON

THE SOUND OF SILENCE

Hello darkness my old friend,
I've come to talk with you again,
Because a vision softly creeping,
Left its seeds while I was sleeping
And the vision that was planted in my brain
Still remains within the sound of silence.

In restless dreams I walked alone,
Narrow streets of cobble stone
'Neath the halo of a street lamp,
I turned my collar to the cold and damp
When my eyes were stabbed by the flash of a neon light
That split the night, and touched the sound of silence.

And in the naked light I saw
Ten thousand people maybe more,
People talking without speaking,
People hearing without listening,
People writing songs that voices never share
And no one dares disturb the sound of silence.

"Fools!" said I, "You do not know
Silence like a cancer grows.
Hear my words that I might teach you
Take my arms that I might reach you."
But my words like silent raindrops fell
And echoed, in the wells of silence.

And the people bowed and prayed
To the neon God they made,
And the sign flashed out its warning
In the words that it was forming.
And the sign said:
   "The words of the prophets are written
   on the subway walls and tenement halls"
And whispered in the sounds of silence.

OLD FRIENDS

Old friends, old friends,
Sat on their park bench
Like bookends.
A newspaper blown through the grass
Falls on the round toes
Of the high shoes
Of the old friends.

Old friends, old friends,
Winter companions,
The old men
Lost in their overcoats,
Waiting for the sunset.
The sounds of the city,
Sifting through trees,
Settle like dust
On the shoulders
Of the old friends.

Can you imagine us
Years from today,
Sharing a park bench quietly?
How terribly strange
To be seventy.

Old Friends, memory brushes the same years.
Silently sharing the same fears.

PETE SEEGER

OH, HAD I A GOLDEN THREAD

Oh, had I a golden thread
And Needle so fine,
I'd weave a magic strand
Of rainbow design,
Of rainbow design.

In it I'd weave the bravery
Of women giving birth,
In it I would weave the innocence
Of children over all the earth,
Children of all earth.

Far over the waters
I'd reach my magic band
Through foreign cities,
To every single land,
To every land.

Show my brothers and sisters
My rainbow design,
Bind up this sorry world
With hand and heart and mind,
Hand and heart and mind.

Far over the waters
I'd reach my magic band
To every human being
So they would understand,
So they'd understand.

Oh, had I a golden thread,
And needle so fine,
I'd weave a magic strand
Of rainbow design,
Of rainbow design.

NINA SIMONE

FOUR WOMEN

My skin is black
My arms are long
My hair is wooly
My back is strong
Strong enough to take the pain
Inflicted again and again
What do they call me?
My name is Aunt Sarah
My name is Aunt Sarah
Aunt Sarah

My skin is yellow
My hair is long
Between two worlds
I do belong
My father was rich and white
He forced my mother late one night
What do they call me?
My name is Saffronia
My name is Saffronia

My skin is tan
My hair is fine
My hips invite you
My mouth like wine
Whose little girl am I?
Anyone who has money to buy
What do they call me?
My name is Sweet Thing
My name is Sweet Thing

My skin is brown
My manner is tough
I'll kill the first mothah I see
My life has been rough
I'm awfully bitter these days
Because my parents were slaves
What do they call me?
My name is . . . PEACHES

A SELECTED DISCOGRAPHY

What follows is designed to help readers locate songs of the poets included here. It is not a complete discography: "singles" are not listed, and frequently only representative albums have been included. The poets are listed alphabetically.

BEATLES

Rubber Soul (Capitol): I've Just Seen a Face; Norwegian Wood; You Won't See Me; Think for Yourself; The Word; Michelle; It's Only Love; Girl; I'm Looking Through You; In My Life; Wait; Run for Your Life

Help! (Capitol): Help!; The Night Before; You've Got to Hide Your Love Away; I Need You; Another Girl; Ticket to Ride; You're Gonna Lose That Girl

Yesterday Today and Tomorrow (Capitol): Drive My Car; I'm Only Sleeping; Nowhere; Dr. Robert; Yesterday; Act Naturally; And Your Bird Can Sing; If I Needed Someone; We Can Work It Out; What Goes On?; Day Tripper

Revolver (Capitol): Taxman; Eleanor Rigby; Love You Too; Here, There and Everywhere; Yellow Submarine; She Said He Said; Good Day Sunshine; For No One; I Want to Tell You; Got to Get You into My Life; Tomorrow Never Knows

Sgt. Pepper's Lonely Hearts Club Band (Capitol): Sgt. Pepper's Lonely Hearts Club Band; A Little Help from My Friends; Lucy in the Sky with Diamonds; Getting Better; Fixing a Hole; She's Leaving Home; Being for the Benefit of Mr. Kite!; Within You Without You; When I'm Sixty-Four; Lovely Rita; Good Morning Good Morning; Sgt. Pepper's Lonely Hearts Club Band (Reprise); A Day in the Life

Magical Mystery Tour (Capitol): Magical Mystery Tour; The Fool on the Hill; Flying; Blueday Way; Your Mother Should Know; I Am the Walrus; Hello Goodbye; Strawberry Fields Forever; Penny Lane; Baby You're a Rich Man; All You Need Is Love

The Beatles (Apple): Back in the U.S.S.R.; Dear Prudence; Glass Onion; Ob-La-Di, Ob-La-Da; Wild Honey Pie; The Continuing Story of Bungalow Bill; While My Guitar Gently Weeps; Happiness Is a Warm Gun; Martha My Dear; I'm So Tired; Blackbird; Piggies; Rocky Racoon; Don't Pass Me By; Why Don't We Do It in the Road?; I Will; Julia; Birthday; Sexy Sadie; Helter Skelter; Long, Long, Long; Revolution 1; Honey Pie; Savoy Truffle; Cry Baby Cry; Revolution 9; Good Night

Abbey Road (Apple): Come Together; Something; Maxwell's Silver Hammer; Oh! Darling; Octopus's Garden; I Want You (She's So Heavy); Here Comes the Sun; Because; You Never Give Me Your Money; Sun King; Mean Mr. Mustard; Polythene Pam; She Came in Through the Bathroom Window; Golden Slumbers; Carry That Weight; The End

JACQUES BREL

Jacques Brel Is Alive and Well and Living in Paris (Columbia): Marathon; Alone; Madeleine; I Loved; Mathilde; Bachelor's Dance; Timid Frieda; My Death;

Jackie; Desperate Ones; Sons of . . . ; Amsterdam; The Bulls; Old Folks; Marieke; Brussels; Fanette; Funeral Tango; You're Not Alone; Next; Carousel; If We Only Have Love

Jacques Brel (Vedettes): J'arrive; Vesoul; L'Ostendaise; Je suis un soir d'été; Regarde bien petit; Comment tuer l'amant de sa femme quand on a été élèvé comme moi dans la tradition; L'Éclusier; Un enfant; La Bière

The Poetic World of Jacques Brel (Phillips): Les prénoms de Paris; Clara; On n'oublie rien; Les singes; La dame patronesse; Seul; Madeleine; Les Biches; Les Paumés du petit matin; Zangra; La Statue; Les Bourgeois

LEONARD COHEN

Songs of Leonard Cohen (Columbia): Suzanne; Master Song; Winter Lady; The Stranger Song; Sisters of Mercy; So Long, Marianne; Hey, That's No Way to Say Goodbye; Stories of the Street; Teachers; One of Us Cannot Be Wrong

Songs from a Room (Columbia): Bird on the Wire; Story of Isaac; A Bunch of Lonesome Heros; The Partisan; Seems So Long Ago, Nancy; The Old Revolution; The Butcher; You Know Who I Am; Lady Midnight; Tonight Will Be Fine

CROSBY, STILLS, AND NASH

Crosby, Stills & Nash (Reprise): Suite: Judy Blue Eyes; Marrakesh Express; Guinnevere; You Don't Have To Cry; Pre-Road Downs; Wooden Ships; Lady of the Island; Helplessly Hoping; Long Time Comin'; 49 Bye-Byes

DONOVAN

Hurdy Gurdy Man (Epic): Hurdy Gurdy Man; Peregrine; The Entertaining of a Shy Girl; As I Recall It; Get Thy Bearings; Hi It's Been a Long Time; West Indian Lady; Jennifer Juniper; The River Song; Tangier; A Sunny Day; The Sun Is a Very Magic Fellow; Teas

A Gift from a Flower to a Garden (Epic): Wear Your Love Like Heaven; Mad John's Escape; Skip-A-Long Sam; Sun; There Was a Time; Oh Gosh; Little Boy in Corduroy; Under the Greenwood Tree; The Land of Doesn't Have to Be; Someone Singing; Song of the Naturalist's Wife; The Enchanted Gypsy; Voyage into the Golden Screen; Isle of Islay; The Mandolin Man and His Secret; Lay of the Last Tinker; The Tinker and the Crab; Widow with Shawl (A Portrait); The Lullaby of Spring; The Magpie; Starfish-on-the-Toast; Epistle to Derroll

Donovan's Greatest Hits (Epic): Mellow Yellow; Sunshine Superman; Hurdy Gurdy Man; Epistle to Dippy; Wear Your Love Like Heaven; Jennifer Juniper; Colours; Catch the Wind; There Is a Mountain; Season of the Witch; Lalena

Barabajagal (Epic): Barabajagal; Superlungs My Supergirl; Where Is She; Happiness Runs; I Love My Shirt; The Love Song; To Susan on the West Coast Waiting; Atlantis; Trudi; Pamela Jo

ARLO GUTHRIE

Alice's Restaurant (Reprise): Alice's Restaurant Massacree; Chilling of the Evening; Ring-Around-a-Rosy Rag; Now and Then; I'm Going Home; The Motorcycle Song; Highway in the Wind

Arlo (Reprise): The Motorcycle Song; Wouldn't You Believe It; Try Me One More Time; John Looked Down; Meditation (Wave upon Wave); Standing at the Threshold; The Pause of Mr. Clause

Original Motion Picture Score—Alice's Restaurant (United Artists): Traveling Music; Alice's Restaurant Massacree, Part I; The Let Down; Songs to Aging Children Come; Amazing Grace; Trip to the City; Alice's Restaurant Massacree, Part 2; Crash Pad Improvs; You're a Fink; Harps and Marriage

Running Down the Road (Reprise): Oklahoma Hills; Every Hand in the Land; Creole Belle; Wheel of Fortune; Oh, in the Morning; Coming into Los Angeles; Stealin'; My Front Pages; Living in the Country; Running Down the Road

TED JOANS

Mr. Joans has been recorded reading his poems, and an album should be available soon on the Motown label.

DON L. LEE

Broadside Press in Detroit has tapes available ($5.00 each) of Mr. Lee reading his book, *Don't Cry, Scream*.

JONI MITCHELL

Joni Mitchell (Reprise): I Had a King; Michael from Mountains; Night in the City; Marcie; Nathan La Franeer; Sisotowbell Lane; The Dawntreader; The Pirate of Penance; Song to a Seagull; Cactus Tree

Clouds (Reprise): Tin Angel; Chelsea Morning; I Don't Know Where I Stand; That Song About the Midway; Roses Blue; The Gallery; I Think I Understand; Songs to Aging Children Come; The Fiddle and the Drum; Both Sides, Now

LAURA NYRO

New York Tendaberry (Columbia): You Don't Love Me When I Cry; Captain for Dark Mornings; Tom Cat Goodbye; Mercy on Broadway; Save the Country; Gibsom Street; Time and Love; The Man Who Sends Me Home; Sweet Lovin Baby; Captain Saint Lucifer; New York Tendaberry

Eli and the Thirteenth Confession (Columbia): Luckie; Lu; Sweet Blindness; Poverty Train; Lonely Women; Eli's Comin; Timer; Stoned Soul Picnic; Emmie; Woman's Blues; Once It Was Alright Now (Farmer Joe); December Boudoir; The Confession

The First Songs of Laura Nyro (Verve-Forecast): Wedding Bell Blues; Billy's Blues; California Shoe Shine Boys; Blowin Away; Lazy Susan; Good Bye Joe; Hands Off the Man (Flim Flam Man); Stoney End; I Never Meant to Hurt You; He's a Runner; Buy and Sell; And When I Die

PHIL OCHS

Phil Ochs in Concert (Elektra): I'm Going to Say It Now; Bracers; Ringing of Revolution; Is There Anybody Here?; Canons of Christianity; There But for Fortune; Cops of the World; Santo Domingo; Changes; Love Me, I'm a Liberal; When I'm Gone

Rehearsals for Retirement (A&M): Pretty Smart on My Part; The Doll House; I Kill Therefore I Am; William Butler Yeats Visits Lincoln Park and Escapes Unscathed; The Scorpion Departs But Never Returns; The World Began in Eden But Ended in Los Angeles; Doesn't Lenny Live Here Anymore?; Another Age; Rehearsals for Retirement

Pleasures of the Harbor (A&M): Cross My Heart; Flower Lady; Outside of a Small Circle of Friends; I've Had Her; Miranda; The Party; Pleasures of the Harbor; The Crucifixion

BUFFY SAINTE-MARIE

Many a Mile (Vanguard): Must I Go Bound; Los Pescadores; Groundhog; On the Banks of Red Roses; Fixin' to Die; Until It's Time for You to Go; The Piney Wood Hills; Welcome Emigrante; Broke-Down Girl; Johnny Be Fair; Maple Sugar Boy; Lazarus; Come All Ye Fair and Tender Girls

I'm Gonna Be a Country Girl Again (Vanguard): I'm Gonna Be a Country Girl Again; He's a Pretty Good Man If You Ask Me; Uncle Joe; A Soulful Shade of Blue; From the Bottom of My Heart; Sometimes When I Get to Thinking; The Piney Wood Hills; Now That the Buffalo's Gone; They Gotta Quit Kicking My Dawg

Around; Tall Trees in Georgia; The Love of a Good Man; Take My Hand for a While; Gonna Feel Much Better When You're Gone

Fire & Fleet & Candlelight (Vanguard): The Seeds of Brotherhood; Summer Boy; The Circle Game; Lyke Wake Dirge; Song to a Seagull; Doggett's Gap; The Wedding Song; 97 Men in This Here Town; Lord Randall; The Carousel; T'es Pas un Autre; Little Boy Dark Eyes; Renardine—A Vampire Legend; Hey, Little Bird

Illuminations (Vanguard): God Is Alive, Magic Is Afoot; Mary; Better to Find Out for Yourself; The Vampire; Adam; The Dream Tree; Suffer the Little Children; The Angel; With You, Honey; Guess Who I Saw in Paris; He's a Keeper of the Fire; Poppies

SIMON AND GARFUNKEL

Sounds of Silence (Columbia): The Sound of Silence; Leaves That Are Green; Blessed; Kathy's Song; Somewhere They Can't Find Me; Angie; Richard Cory; A Most Peculiar Man; April Come She Will; We've Got a Groovy Thing Goin'; I Am a Rock

Wednesday Morning, 3 a.m. (Columbia): You Can Tell the World; Last Night I Had the Strangest Dream; Bleecker Street; Sparrow; Benedictus; The Sound of Silence; He Was My Brother; Peggy-O; Go Tell It on the Mountain; The Sun Is Burning; The Times They Are A-Changing; Wednesday Morning, 3 a.m.

Parsley, Sage, Rosemary and Thyme (Columbia): Scarborough Fair/Canticle; Patterns; For Emily, Wherever I May Find Her; The Big Bright Green Pleasure Machine; A Poem on the Underground Wall; Cloudy; A Simple Desultory Philippic/or How I Was Robert McNamara'd into Submission; The 59th Street Bridge Song (Feelin' Groovy); Flowers Never Bend with the Rainfall; 7 O'Clock News/ Silent Night

Bookends (Columbia): Bookends Theme; Save the Life of My Child; America; Overs; Voices of Old People; Old Friends; Bookends Theme; Fakin It; Punky's Dilemma; Mrs. Robinson; A Hazy Shade of Winter; At the Zoo

NINA SIMONE

The Best of Nina Simone (Columbia): I Loves You, Porgy; Mississippi Goddam; Sinnerman; See-Line Woman; I Put a Spell on You; Break Down & Let It All Out; Four Women; Wild Is the Wind; Pirate Jenny; Don't Let Me Be Misunderstood